Norman Miller

111 Places
in Chichester
and West Sussex
That You
Shouldn't Miss

emons:

Bibliographical information of the Deutsche Nationalbibliothek
The Deutsche Nationalbibliothek lists this publication in
the Deutsche Nationalbibliografie; detailed bibliographical data
are available on the internet at http://dnb.d-nb.de.

© Emons Verlag GmbH
All rights reserved
© Photographs by Norman Miller, except: see page 238
© Cover icon: mauritius images/Graham Prentice/Alamy/Alamy Stock Photos
Coverdesign: Karolin Meinert
Layout: Eva Kraskes, based on a design
by Lübbeke | Naumann | Thoben
Maps: altancicek.design, www.altancicek.de
Basic cartographical information from Openstreetmap,
© OpenStreetMap-Mitwirkende, OdbL
Edited by: Martin Sketchley
Printing and binding: Grafisches Centrum Cuno, Calbe
Printed in Germany 2024
ISBN 978-3-7408-1784-8
First edition

Guidebooks for Locals & Experienced Travellers
Join us in uncovering new places around the world at
www.111places.com

Foreword

It's not hard to see why the Romans founded Chichester where they did around A.D. 43. Christened Noviomagus Reginorum and ruled by a commander who later became the Emperor Vespasian, this ancient walled town sits at the apex of a superb natural harbour reaching deep into England's south coast, backed by a breathtaking hinterland that became England's newest 21st-century National Park.

Though now flanked by larger, more modern towns such as Littlehampton and Bognor Regis, Chichester remains pre-eminent at the heart of West Sussex, the county capital and seat of a 1,000-year-old bishopric whose bustling streets lined with Georgian buildings radiate from a medieval market cross. To the east, Arundel provides a gorgeous complement, mixing medieval roots with a sense of independent style and a thriving local arts scene.

Magnificent aristocratic houses at Petworth, Parham and Goodwood – and evocative ruins at Cowdray – are crucibles of fascinating history, offering Turner masterpieces, sporting icons and ancient curses, and a Wendy House big enough to walk in!

To the south, a very different landscape beckons, combining the atmospheric reed-fringed shores of Chichester Harbour with hidden gems dotting the strikingly named Manhood Peninsula, once a proud Saxon kingdom.

Sussex is underpinned by its own idiosyncratic style – captured in the region's ancient motto 'We wunt de druv' ('We will not be driven'). Despite the pride, it's a place that doesn't always boast about its attractions. Let this book be your guide to see it with fresh eyes.

111 Places

1 Amberley Museum

A wild wander through the working past

For over a century, from the 1840s to 1960s, this was a working chalk quarry extending over 36 acres in the heart of the South Downs. Transformed into one of Britain's finest outdoor museums in the late 1970s, Amberley Museum offers an inspiring exploration of historic industries, transport and traditional crafts in a natural sylvan setting.

Alongside vintage industrial infrastructure (old kilns, giant engines), historic buildings have been repurposed to highlight different areas of working heritage. A delightful narrow gauge miniature railway and a 100-year-old bus provide memorable transport around the site.

The 40-plus exhibition areas are impressively diverse. Discover how birch brooms have been made in Sussex since Saxon times, then check out a 1930s cobbler's shop relocated from its former location in Bognor Regis. Fans of vintage technology can reminisce over fabulous old phones, radios and TVs, whilst learning how communication evolved from the first Morse code transmission to modern computer chips. Even better, old kit is put to use through activities such as the Museum's own radio station, or the 1930s rural telephone exchange that still handles its internal calls.

There's also a thought-provoking Hidden Innovators exhibition, which spotlights women and people from black and minority ethnic backgrounds, who were denied due recognition for their pioneering technology achievements. They include black electrical engineer Rufus Paul Turner, who developed the first practical transistor radio in 1949, and Erna Schneider Hoover, who in the 1950s became the first woman to receive a computer software patent. James Bond film fans, meanwhile, should head for the old quarry tunnel near the Museum's 'Brockham Station', where Roger Moore and Grace Jones foiled the bad guys when it served as Mainstrike Mine in the 1980s blockbuster *A View To A Kill*.

Address New Barn Road, Amberley, BN18 9LT, amberleymuseum.co.uk | Getting there The Museum is directly opposite Amberley railway station; by car, 12 miles north-east of Chichester at Houghton Bridge, via the B2139 | Hours Feb–Oct Wed–Sun 10am–4.30pm, plus Bank Holidays; Nov–Jan Wed, Sat & Sun 10am–4pm; some Christmas/New Year closures | Tip The outdoor terrace at the Riverside Tea Rooms is a lovely spot for drinks and light meals and long views beside the banks of the River Arun just 100 metres from the museum. For a pub lunch, meanwhile, the Bridge Inn, just across the road, offers a Mediterranean-influenced menu.

2__ Francis Wood Tomb

Remembering a forgotten hero of medicine

By a wall beside ancient yews at St Michael's Church in Amberley is a memorial to the man behind a pioneering rehabilitation project for wounded World War I soldiers dubbed the 'Tin Noses Shop' – which medical history records as the 'Masks for Facial Disfigurement Department', set up by Francis Derwent Wood at the 3rd London General Hospital in 1915.

Wood was a noted sculptor rather than a medical practitioner. When war broke out in 1914 he volunteered for combat, but being in his early 40s was rejected due to age. Signing up instead for hospital work, he was confronted with the devastating injuries being suffered on the battlefield. He also became aware of the particular psychological and social impact of facial disfigurement, which often led to victims being shunned by society.

For those for whom reconstructive surgery was impossible, Wood set up a team to create tailor-made masks that drew on pre-war photographs to recreate the patient's face in as natural looking a way as possible. A plaster cast was taken of the subject's wounded face after surgeries were complete and healed, and the resulting plaster mould then used to make a mask from thin copper sheets. This was painstakingly painted, and finished off while being worn by the patient, in order to match their flesh tone. Each mask required many weeks of work.

Wood's unit transformed the lives of hundreds of disfigured veterans before being disbanded when peace came in 1918. He said: 'The patient acquires his old self-respect, self-assurance, self-reliance, and, discarding his induced despondency, takes once more to a pride in his personal appearance.'

Wood went on to become Professor of Sculpture at the Royal College of Art, as well as making public art works such as *The Boy David* at London's Hyde Park Corner, dedicated to the Machine Gun Corps. He also created the bronze pietà bas-relief on his own tomb.

·DERWENT·WOOD·1909·

Address St Michael's Church, Church Street, Amberley, BN18 9ND,
www.achurchnearyou.com/church/4758 | Getting there 30-minute walk from Amberley
railway station (you can cut through the grounds of Amberley Castle past the tennis
courts); by car via the B 2139, 15 miles from Chichester | Hours Churchyard accessible
24 hours | Tip The Black Horse is a cosy village pub a few hundred metres from
the church, decorated with vintage panache and offering a field-to-fork local menu
(www.amberleyblackhorse.co.uk).

3 Arundel Lido
The best swimming pool view in England?

Views from the clear blue waters of the lovely open-air pool at Arundel Lido must make it difficult for swimmers to concentrate on their stroke, given an eyeline filled with one of England's most beautiful panoramas – the ravishing medieval town of Arundel, spread across a meadow-wrapped hill topped by England's biggest castle.

Despite its Sussex location, Arundel Castle is the dazzling home of the Duke of Norfolk. It was a donation of land from the then Duke in 1960 – to mark the 21st birthday of his eldest daughter, Lady Anne – that provided the site on which the first Arundel Lido was built. Today's Lido – consisting of a 25-metre heated main pool and a 5-metre splash pool – is the only one remaining in West Sussex. The original 1960s pool was given a bold makeover in 2000 by the award-winning Adam Richards Architects, who took inspiration for their design from the discovery of a nearby Roman villa. Drawing on the history of public baths from antiquity, the changing room features brick walls that ripple as if seen through water, plus a two-storey wing hosting 'civic' spaces oriented to point like an arrow from town into the beautiful surrounding countryside.

The Lido is run by a community trust that arranges a busy programme of activities. These include a Community Cuppa, designed to help people who feel isolated, or those suffering from dementia, to socialise with others over a hot drink and snacks. Although the Lido's main open season is geared to the warmer months of the year, from May to September, the pool also stages traditional Festive Swims on Christmas Eve, Christmas Day, Boxing Day, New Year's Eve and New Year's Day – for those hardy swimmers wanting to mix warm water with freezing air! The ongoing Project LEAP promises new developments, including a gym and multi-purpose community hall and café, aiming to make Arundel Lido a year-round pleasure.

Address Queen Street, Arundel, BN18 9JG, www.arundel-lido.com | **Getting there** 15-minute walk from Arundel railway station | **Hours** Mon 6.30am–7.45pm, Tue & Thu 7.30am–9pm, Wed 6.30am–8pm, Fri 6.30am–6.30pm, Sat 8am–6pm, Sun 9am–6pm | **Tip** Arundel offers a more wild watery place for fun at Swanbourne Lake, around a 30-minute stroll along nearby Mill Lane. Hire a rowing boat or just watch the waterfowl from the lakeside Swanbourne Lodge tearoom (www.swanbournelodgetearoom.co.uk).

4 Demon Trap
Beautiful geometry with supernatural roots

St Nicholas Church has been part of Arundel's striking hilltop town-scape since 1380, serving as the town's parish church to both Roman Catholic and Anglican communities. Most attention goes to the grand Fitzalan Chapel, visible through a wrought iron grille – off limits to the general congregation as a place of worship due to being set aside for the aristocratic occupiers of England's largest castle, next door to the church. Another feature that gets attention is the faded medieval wall paintings over the north door, depicting the seven deadly sins and the seven works of mercy.

But a fascinating mark of ancient beliefs missed by almost every visitor beckons on an ancient stone pillar between the pipes of the church's organ and the Fitzalan Chapel iron grille. Look closely about head height, and you see a petalled flower pattern scratched onto the stone – a Demon Trap!

Belief in demonic evil spirits was very real in medieval times (and for centuries after). Demons were blamed for ill-luck, illness or other personal disasters. Drawing demon traps as a form of protection arose from the idea that these evil spirits, though malevolent, had a curiosity that could be exploited. If they came across a line, they would follow it to see where it led. But if the line was drawn so as to have no conclusion – as in a repeating shape – the demon would be 'trapped' going round and round within the symbol.

The concept has roots in the Old Testament tale of King Solomon being given a signet ring by the Archangel Michael inscribed with a magical seal, among whose powers was one to command demons. The ring allegedly bore a magical shape, most commonly depicted as a Star of David or pentagram. By the time our Demon Trap was drawn, this had expanded to include petal shapes or knotted designs. The key was a geometry to trap demons in eternal pursuit of never-ending lines.

Address St Nicholas Parish Church, London Road, Arundel, BN18 9AT, www.stnicholas-arundel.co.uk | Getting there 25-minute walk from Arundel railway station | Hours Daily 9am–5pm | Tip Fans of supernatural symbols should head for Binsted, three miles south-west of Arundel, to see a striking wooden memorial sculpted by Janine Creaye beside the village church, celebrating the local legend of dragon-like spirits reputed to live deep in a 'bottomless' pond in the village.

5 Gallery 57
Natural materials transformed into dazzling art

This outstanding Arundel contemporary gallery opened in 2016 inside the Georgian house of artist Ann Symes, who relocated from her previous studio home surrounded by Sussex woodland. The residential setting gives the space a welcoming air for its regularly changing displays of often dazzling contemporary craft-based artworks.

Local, national and international artists and makers underpin the regularly changing programme of thoughtfully curated, themed exhibitions. More importantly, the gallery specifically showcases artists adopting often hugely innovative working methods based on unusual materials and techniques. By placing importance on how work is displayed and given space, it also creates the calm aesthetic that encourages visitors to explore and linger. Engagement is further encouraged by a chance to browse leading craft magazines.

Ann's studio is linked to the gallery where she sometimes works when the gallery is open – though she is always on hand to answer questions. The studio space also hosts one-day workshops run by expert tutors and makers, and the gallery has a strong online presence that promotes worldwide connections.

Gallery 57 has a particularly striking focus on work made with what it broadly classes as 'earth materials'. These include the stunning found-oak works of both Alison Crowther and Philip Walker, Claire Benn's textiles dyed with earth pigments, and intricate paper-pulp works fashioned by Jane Ponsford. Meanwhile, the dazzling basketry created by Annette Mills – looped, braided or woven vessels integrating bark, foraged flowers and grasses – is partly inspired by Iceland's traditional turf houses.

Symes' own work stands out too, and includes a 2017 project which brilliantly brought together charcoal drawing with intricate sculptural folding in a way that explored both formal structure and memories of childhood games.

Address 57 Tarrant Street, Arundel, BN18 9DJ, www.gallery57.co.uk | Getting there 20-minute walk from Arundel railway station | Hours Tue–Sat 11am–4pm, Sun noon–4pm | Tip A fine complement to the object-based works at Gallery 57, the nearby Arundel Contemporary gallery showcases an interesting range of British and international painting and print works (www.arundelcontemporary.com).

6 Lime Trees Project
Wartime arboreal memories – with promise of a kiss

The double avenue of trees along Mill Road in Arundel is the UK's only publicly accessible double avenue of lime trees, and was planted in honour of the road's creation by the Duke of Norfolk estate in 1894. Intended to provide a route to nearby Swanbourne Lake and farms beyond, the thoroughfare was then simply known as New Road. And despite the English name, it should be noted that these are not citrus fruit lime trees, but rather the species known as linden in European countries such as Germany.

The original tree planting had intended to alternate lime and alder trees along its quarter-mile original length, with the idea that the presence of alders would encourage the lime trees to grow taller in search of sunlight! This idea was soon abandoned, however, and all the alders were removed. The original lime trees were common lime (*Tilia europaea*) but in recent times the small leafed lime (*Tilia cordata*) has been preferred, as they do not annually sprout new growth around the base of each tree that has to be removed (at significant expense). However, a bonus with the original Victorian trees is that common lime attracts the parasitic growth of mistletoe, which is harvested today for Christmas kissing traditions!

The people of Arundel continue to add young lime trees, most recently in 2020 when 34 small leafed lime were planted. Saplings are grown in the Netherlands, and the purchase of each new tree is sponsored by a local resident. Local schoolchildren also get involved in the planting of new trees, with each one bearing a different child's name.

With a lifespan of up to three centuries, the older lime trees have borne witness to passing years as well as passing cars. The most notable mementoes are carvings made in the trunks by US and Canadian soldiers who massed beneath the lime trees during preparations for the D-Day landings in 1944.

Address Mill Road, Arundel, BN18 9PA | **Getting there** Train to Arundel railway station, then a 10-minute walk | **Hours** Accessible 24 hours | **Tip** Tree lovers can also admire a pair of beautiful magnolias beside the ancient gate to Arundel Castle at the beginning of the lime tree avenue. The limes also feature in an audio tour entitled *The Notable Trees of Arundel*, available via www.visitarundel.co.uk.

7 __ Nineveh House
A vintage cornucopia building with a mysterious name

This characterful antiques and craft centre provides an Arundel beacon for worshippers of distinctive style – home to diverse independent traders and specialist artisans selling everything from vintage gramophones to studio glass and woodwork. For much of its history, though, this served as a place for more traditional worship.

The history of the site goes back much further to a mansion called Nineveh House, built around 1420 for the 13th Earl of Arundel, John Fitzalan. The house was constructed largely with chalk, and faced with flint, key local materials found on the surrounding South Downs. The two sandstone pillars greeting present-day visitors at the entrance to Nineveh House are believed to be all that remains of the original mansion, marking the entrance to grounds that stretched down to the River Arun. A waning of fortunes for a family who once claimed the magnificent nearby Arundel Castle saw the mansion abandoned, and left to decay. At various points through the 17th and 18th centuries it was rented out as space for stores and workshops. For a time, it also hosted a drinking establishment called the Star Inn. Eventually, the old Nineveh House was demolished.

The arrival of a group of independent-thinking Christians in Arundel saw them construct their own chapel further along Tarrant Street – though their presence stirred up controversies. For example, one of their members – a preacher called George MacDonald – was deemed to espouse such unconventional views in his moral and mystical writings that he was forced to leave Arundel! Still, the congregation thrived, and in 1836 bought the site of today's Nineveh House to build what became known as the Arundel Independent Church. But no-one knows why the original mansion was named after one of humanity's oldest cities, the ancient Assyrian capital on the Tigris River in what is now Iraq.

Address 31a Tarrant Street, Arundel, BN18 9DG | Getting there 30-minute walk from Arundel railway station | Hours Daily 9.30am–4.30pm (except Christmas Day and New Year's Day) | Tip Look above the shop front of the neighbouring Larkin's grocery shop to see a blue plaque commemorating the original siting of the former chapel.

8__ Oberon's Palace
A magical balancing act with history

The most ornate spot in Arundel Castle's expansive grounds is The Collector Earl's Garden, designed in 2008 by Isobel and Julian Bannerman in tribute to Thomas Howard, 14th Earl of Arundel (1585–1646). He acquired his 'Collector' tag after amassing over 700 paintings and other cultural souvenirs on the European 'Grand Tour' popular with the wealthy of the time. The Garden's most eye-popping centrepiece is Oberon's Palace.

Rather than anything outwardly grand, this 'palace' looks more like a humble little folly, fashioned from green oak and set on a little mound. The approach to this strange hillock temple, through palm trees and ferns, suggests something more exotic, however. It's only up close that the startling beauty of its interior is revealed – a magical watery grotto decorated with cockle shells, inset with a mosaic of vases and orange trees made from broken mussel shells. The hypnotic centrepiece is a fountain designed so that a gilded coronet 'dances' ceaselessly in mid-air, as it jitters around on top of an upward jet of water.

The historical inspiration of Oberon's Palace was a fantasy theatrical set created by famed architect designer Inigo Jones for a celebratory masque – a lavish entertainment blending music, dance and written performance – held on New Year's Day, 1611, for a royal visit by Prince Henry Frederick, eldest son of James I. Words for the *The Masque of Oberon* performed that day were written by illustrious 17th-century playwright Ben Jonson, a friend – and rival – of Shakespeare.

It's not recorded how *The Masque of Oberon* was received by guests, but the young prince who watched it was fated never to become king, dying of typhoid just a year after his Arundel visit. A unique fountain with a golden crown whirling around atop fluctuating support perhaps offers a resonant image of the ephemeral nature of power faced with life.

Address Arundel Castle, Arundel, BN18 9AB, www.arundelcastle.org | **Getting there**
15-minute walk from Arundel railway station | **Hours** Gardens Mon–Sat 10am–5pm | **Tip**
Visit a beautiful historic folly in the shape of the Hiorne Tower (BN18 9AU), a mile north
of Arundel Castle; built in 1797 by Francis Hiorne to showcase his workmanship as part
of a bid for a rebuilding contract at the castle, it was left abandoned when he didn't get the
job – but it did appear in an episode of cult BBC TV series *Doctor Who*!

9__ Old Print Works
Fine retro shopping in storied surrounds

Not many shopping arcades get Grade II-listed historic building status, but the spot that now hosts a fascinating community of small independent local Arundel businesses has a past as intriguing as the diverse wares on offer inside.

The Old Print Works takes its name from its long-time past role as the home of the West Sussex Gazette. The first edition of what remains Sussex's oldest regional newspaper was published here in 1853. Copies of the paper were typeset and hand-printed on a large Eagle Hand Press, with each letter carefully placed by hand, back to front, to form a word that could then be printed. A fire that devastated the building in March 1889 led to a rebuilding effort that not only created the Jacobean style / Sussex half timber edifice that greets people today, but resulted in the building being hailed by *The British Architect* journal as 'the most artistic county newspaper office… in England'. In 1996, however, the newspaper's printing rooms moved to Portsmouth, while its editorial team relocated to Chichester, where the *West Sussex Gazette* is still put together today.

There's still a vintage vibe to several of the businesses in the Old Print Works. Retroesque is a beacon for vintage fashion from the 1920s–1950s, which unusually also offers a good selection of retro menswear on its first floor. Milliner Isabella Josie, meanwhile, creates bespoke hats and fascinators inspired by 1940s/50s style which work wonderfully for vintage events such as August's Goodwood Revival. You can also scour vintage vinyl records at A Ray of Delight, pick up retro gifts and memorabilia at AJ's Emporium, or get a stylish haircut at Golden Blade vintage barber shop. And if you're ever keen to make a movie in Sussex, this is also the place to get information and permits from the Sussex Film Office, based at Unit 16 (www.sussexfilmoffice.co.uk).

Address Old Printing House Square, Tarrant Street, Arundel, BN18 9JH, www.oldprintworksarundel.co.uk | Getting there 20-minute walk from Arundel railway station | Hours Varies from shop to shop but generally 9am–5pm | Tip You can see some of the 19th-century printing presses used for the West Sussex Gazette at the nearby Arundel Museum (www.arundelmuseum.org).

10 Pollinators' Garden

Bringing an inspiring buzz to Arundel

In 2019, Arundel resident – and beekeeper – Nick Field started a community drive to encourage a shared appreciation of bees and the vital role they play in nature as pollinators. His ultimate aim is for Arundel to be declared 'The UK's first bee-friendly town' via a project that has drawn together hundreds of local people.

'Pollinators play a vital role in the production of about one third of the food we eat,' Field told Sussex World. 'With their numbers in sharp decline, it's essential that we do all we can to provide them with sources of food and shelter.' The most visible result of the project's work so far is the lovely Pollinators' Garden created in 2021 on land opposite the Arundel Museum – where an old public toilet block once stood. Here, a team led by Arundel Castle head gardener Martin Duncan created a bee-friendly miniature Eden in a vibrant patch of greenery, which also opens up views of Arundel Castle and the historic Blackfriars Ruins – the remains of a Dominican friary dating back to the 13th century.

Elsewhere, several hives now buzz with life on the Community Apiary site in Arundel Community Orchard at Herington's Field. In 2022, meanwhile, volunteers cleared weeds, nettles and overgrown grass bordering the path to Arundel Station, and sowed thousands of wildflower seeds to create a far better environment not just for pollinator bees and butterflies, but human users too. The project also issues ongoing calls for people to create their own mini contributions – be it hosting a hive, learning to be a beekeeper, or coming up with ideas for bee-friendly events, bee art, or selling bee-related products.

Field sees the Arundel project as providing a template for other Bee-Friendly towns. 'If this is a success, it could be launched throughout the UK in future years,' he said. 'However, Arundel would always be the first one.'

Address The garden is opposite Arundel Museum, Mill Road, Arundel, BN18 9PA; the project also has an office at 44 Tarrant Street, Arundel, BN18 9DN, www.arundelbeeproject.org | Getting there 20-minute walk from Arundel railway station | Hours Pollinators' Garden and Arundel Community Orchard accessible 24 hours | Tip Buy Sussex-produced honey from the Arundel Farmers Market, held in the Town Hall on every third Saturday (www.arundelfarmersmarket.co.uk).

11_Poor Clares of Arundel

The tranquil home of chart-topping holy sisters

The Catholic roots of the Poor Clares date back to the 1200s, with each convent enjoying a degree of autonomy in how its sisters live. And in Arundel, this saw the recording of an album that made these Sussex sisters the UK's best-selling artist debut of 2020!

As the UK faced the COVID pandemic, Arundel's Poor Clares decided to record an album of plainsong featuring Latin and Medieval hymns. Entitled *Light for the World* and released in October 2020, its aim was to offer 'joy and energy' at a time of societal stress, as well as providing what one sister described as 'a good adventure'. The calm beauty of the music clearly struck a chord, as the album soared to the top of the UK Classical music charts, where it stayed for 19 weeks!

It was a wonderful boost for a community that endured a difficult beginning. In August 1886, 10 Poor Clares from a community in London took the train to Arundel to found a new outpost at the request of Flora, Duchess of Norfolk, on land provided by her and her ducal husband – owners of the town's epic castle. But when the duchess died in early 1887, the sisters were left struggling grievously without a benefactor. Two died of consumption, and five of the remaining sisters left. The community grew during the 20th century, however. A wild area was turned into a sustaining garden, and numbers were boosted by amalgamations, such as the 1970s influx of Franciscan sisters of the Third Order Regular Enclosed from Berkshire.

There are just over 20 sisters here today, combining daily prayer with producing craft work for sale in the convent shop. Items include hand-painted icons, wood turning, knitted garments, candles and wax cards. And for anyone wanting to experience life here, there's also a convent guesthouse, where anyone can ask to stay in return for a donation covering lunch with the sisters, as well as a bed.

Address Crossbush Lane, Crossbush, Arundel, BN18 9PJ, www.poorclaresarundel.org |
Getting there The Convent is 500 metres from Arundel railway station; just outside
Arundel via the A27 | **Hours** Visitors welcome to attend scheduled prayers throughout
the day, beginning with Morning Prayer at 7.30am and ending with Night Prayer at 8pm;
there are also annual events, particularly around Easter and Christmas | **Tip** Take a walk
along Crossbush Lane – running off the A27 between the Poor Clares convent and Arundel
station – to get one of the finest views over fields to Arundel's magnificent castle and
cathedral-studded skyline.

12 Priory Playhouse
Modern drama staged in medieval hideaway

The soaring flint walls that hold this charming 78-seat theatre were once the west wing of Arundel Priory, completed in 1380, which makes Priory Playhouse Britain's second-oldest operating theatre building, beaten only by Winchester's Chesil Theatre (hosted inside a church dating back to 1148).

The Priory flourished until the 16th century, when Henry VIII declared himself head of the Church of England in order to both consolidate power, and seize church property and wealth for his own ends. While many priories, abbeys and other religious buildings were sadly destroyed, the Arundel site was handed over to the then 12th Earl of Arundel. The building's respite was only temporary, however, as the English Civil War, a century later, saw it severely damaged. It was left to lie in ruins for much of the next three centuries.

It was the 11th Duke of Norfolk who restored what was left of the building, with the spruced-up west end becoming a public Oratory space for local Catholics. The 14th Duke kept up the building's reinvention, making it into a convent space during the 1800s, inside which the sisters ran a small school that became known as 'The Priory', which ran until 1960. Around this time, the recently-formed Arundel Players (established in 1959) began performing at a church hall run by what is now the present-day Cathedral, but found themselves homeless in 1965 when that space was no longer available. At which point, Lavinia, Duchess of Norfolk – who also happened to be President of the acting company – helped the Players negotiate a lease with the Knights of Malta to turn the derelict Oratory into a theatre.

The conversion – using plans by Neill Holland, an architect who was also an actor – made no real changes to the fabric of this historic space, which opened for its first performances in 1977 and now stages around a dozen diverse productions each year.

Address St Wilfred's Priory, London Road, Arundel, BN18 9AT, www.arundelplayers.co.uk | Getting there Train to Arundel railway station, then a 25-minute walk | Hours The Playhouse opens an hour before performances, which are usually at 7.30pm | Tip For a fine local theatrical complement, check out productions by the Drip Action Theatre (www.dripaction.com), who combine staging modern work at the nearby Victoria Institute with atmospheric summertime productions in the rural setting of Chapel Barn in South Stoke.

13 Spencer Swaffer Antiques

A shop owner as fabled as his wares

Based in Arundel for half a century, Spencer Swaffer is an international legend of the antiques trade, with a back story as fascinating as the dazzling array of objects he sells to both casual drop-ins and international stars – such as six marble urns that went to Tina Turner's French villa. His shop is carved from a huge, rambling building that is an impressive antique in itself, dating back to 1590 when it hosted a pub called the George Tavern.

Swaffer's own story is a tale to share over a drink. It begins when, aged 11 and living in Brighton, he set up his own museum, charging two pence to anyone wanting to see old objects he had found or bought in junk shops. The museum led to an interview on BBC Radio 4's Today programme, prompting a visit by a curious Brighton antique dealer. When they offered £50 for some Egyptian pottery, the canny boy instantly converted from museum curator to budding antiques dealer! He opened his first antique shop in Brighton, aged just 16.

Before then, he recalls forging a quirky partnership with a girl from his school who 'became a man (and) grew a handlebar moustache… We made quite a strange pair'. Every weekend, the duo drove to London to sell wares in Camden Passage. After leaving school, he enrolled on a journalism course in Portsmouth, due to his parents pleading with him to find a 'proper' career. But when they both died when he was aged only 20, Swaffer used his inheritance to buy the shop in Arundel. The rest, like his wares, is history.

Speaking to *Antiques Trade Gazette*, Swaffer reflected on his unusual start. 'I used to roam the Downs, picking up shards of pottery, fossilised sea urchins… anything that was a bit weird.' That one-time young Sussex Downs explorer continues to hunt across Europe in search of amazing things that draw buyers to Arundel from across the globe.

Address 30 High Street, Arundel, BN18 9AB, www.spencerswaffer.co.uk | Getting there Train to Arundel railway station, then a 20-minute walk | Hours Mon–Sat 9am–5pm | Tip Another outlet of note is Arundel Eccentrics, whose old warehouse offers a diverse collection of English and French decorative antiques; check website to arrange a visit (www.arundeleccentrics.com).

14 Tea and Biscuit Club

A refreshing and exotic taste of the world

This shrine to tea was founded by Erik and Faye Childerhouse, following careers leading international development projects across the globe. Their shop takes inspiration from that past life, drawing on travels to over 90 countries during the last 20 years to inspire their expanding array of blends, encompassing white, black and green teas, fruit blends and herbal infusions.

Around 60 blends are currently available, arrayed in giant jars to tempt customers looking for a scoop of leafy colour to brighten up the traditional British cuppa. As well as their own classic English Breakfast, there is a host of innovative options to try. Turmeric Vanilla Chia or Tropical Oolong, perhaps? Or how about naturally fermented Orange Pu-Erh? Many of the blends come with a story attached, which Erik and Faye are happy to share from behind the counter. The teas have regularly received the UK's prestigious Great Taste Awards too. Past winners include Rooibos Rhubarb Pie – South African rooibos underlaid with rhubarb, cherries, cranberries and apples – and Raspberry Parfair, a caffeine-free infusion bursting with bright flavours, including elderberry, lavender and hibiscus.

Inspired by their international development backgrounds, Erik and Faye also donate some of their proceeds each year to the charity Shine (www.shinecharity.org), which tackles childhood illiteracy in southern Africa, as well as providing vital school meals to malnourished pupils. The shop also sells a range of teapots from old-school shapes in zingy colours (purple pot, anyone?) to designer square glass pots, and brightly patterned heart-shaped pots!

Erik and Faye also run private tea tastings for 2–10 people (£25 per person) between April and October in the shop's walled garden beside Arundel Castle, offering the chance to sample up to biscuits. Green & Coal cafe also serves the shop's teas in a retro setting just metres away.

Address 26 High Street, Arundel, BN18 9AB, www.theteaandbiscuitclub.com | **Getting there** 20-minute walk from Arundel railway station | **Hours** Daily 9am–5.30pm | **Tip** Combine a tea sampling with something stronger, with a sparkling wine tasting across the road at Digby Fine English. One-hour tastings also offer a perfect chance to try the globally renowned local Sussex sparkling wine (www.digby-fine-english.com).

15 — Victoria Institute

Banking on an inspiring community arts future

When the Arundel Savings Bank opened here in 1847, on the site of two former cottages, its owners can have had little idea of the future uses their gorgeous white edifice would serve. What is often known locally simply as The Vic has been, among other things, a snooker hall, laundry, library and dance hall. For the past decade, though, The Vic has become an evolving 21st-century cultural centre, with a programme showcasing the Akin creative collective (www.akinarundel.com), contemporary drama group Drip Action Theatre (www.dripaction.co.uk), the Boathouse Ballet School for children, and Frances Knight's contemporary gallery space (www.francesknight.com).

Perhaps due to having to vie for local money with one of Victorian Arundel's busiest pubs directly opposite, the bank closed in 1896, with the building sold to Arundel Borough Council, who renamed it The Victoria Institute to mark the 60th anniversary of Queen Victoria's reign in 1897. With a desire to 'better working folk', its interior was carved into reading rooms where newspapers were laid out, complemented by a public laundry and bathhouse. From 1925, the building housed a new Country Library Service. These worthy activities, however, were superseded after World War II when the reading room made way for pool and snooker tables, while what is now the Red Room became a bar, then a dance hall.

Despite the grand frontage gaining Grade II-listed status in 1971, changing entertainment patterns saw The Vic's usage dwindle, and the fabric of the building decayed until closure loomed. But in 2014, a volunteer group raised funds to buy the building and begin its return as an inspirational social hub for the town. Working to a plan created by award-winning Tony Fretton Architects, there are plans to add a cinema as well as new courtyard and back garden spaces to The Vic, all whilst espousing carbon-neutral principles.

Address 10 Tarrant Street, Arundel, BN18 9DG, www.thevictoriainstitute.com | Getting there Train to Arundel railway station, then a 20-minute walk | Hours 9am–late evening, depending on events | Tip If you're looking for atmospheric nightlife in Arundel, check out the Arundel Jailhouse – a unique, and reputedly haunted, venue carved from the 1830s former Town Hall Prison (www.arundeljailhouse.co.uk).

16 — Blake's Cottage
Birthplace of one of England's most famous poems

Though he only lived with his wife Catherine in this cottage in the coastal village of Felpham for a few years, from 1800 to 1803, William Blake penned some of his most famous work here. This included the opening of the famous hymn *Jerusalem* from his epic poem *Milton*, among the most famous sentences in English literature: 'And did those feet in ancient time / Walk upon England's mountains green?'

Blake revealed a particular fondness for this 18th-century Grade II-listed brick and flint cottage, praising its 'thatched roof of rusted gold', and writing that 'no other house can please me so well, nor shall I ever be persuaded, I believe, that it can ever be improved in beauty or use'. The poet also had admiring words for Felpham, writing of 'sweet air and the voices of winds, trees, and birds, and the odours of the happy ground'.

The reason Blake quit this seaside idyll was an incident when he became involved in a drunken row with a soldier outside the nearby Fox Inn, when the soldier accused the poet of saying 'Damn the King!'. This alleged outburst saw Blake charged with treason and put on trial for his life at Chichester Guildhall. Though acquitted, the incident soured Blake's life in Felpham, and he left in 1803 to spend the rest of his life in London.

The house was bought for the nation in 2015 by The Blake Cottage Trust, which is now raising funds to restore it to its 18th-century prime, in time for the 200th anniversary of Blake's death in 2027. This will include installing replicas of Blake's printing and engraving presses, and creating a space for resident creatives to work. There will also be open day access to the public – although people can already visit the historic garden on certain days. Until then, just admire its beauty from outside – and raise a (peaceful) glass to toast a great poet/artist at the still bustling Fox Inn.

Address Blakes Road, Bognor Regis, PO22 7EE, www.blakecottage.org | Getting there
The prettiest approach is walking along the Bognor Regis seafront promenade, then turning
inland at Felpham Sailing Club on to Blakes Road; the cottage is a 45-minute walk from
Bognor Regis railway station; or take bus 700 towards Elmer from Bognor Regis High
Street | Hours Exterior accessible 24 hours | Tip Just a 5-minute walk down to the seafront
you find a perfect photo opportunity with a long line of bright yellow-and-blue-painted
beach huts along Felpham Beach.

17 _ Bognor Museum
Charming treasure trove of past local life

Bognor Museum – set up and run by volunteers from the Bognor Regis Local History Society – provides heartening proof of the old saying 'small is beautiful'. The museum focuses mainly on various aspects of social history from the time when Sir Richard Hotham set about transforming a small fishing village into a fashionable seaside resort. This includes a scale model of Sir Richard's home, Hotham Park House, in recognition of his key influence on the town. That's complemented by a beautiful scale model of the Esplanade Theatre, which once stood nearby.

The museum's displays are pleasingly diverse, with lovingly curated exhibits covering music, archaeology, science and technology, toys and hobbies, photography, old shops and fashion. One stand-out room showcases the wonderfully evocative Ron Simpson Wireless Collection, brought together by a former curator with a passion for old radios. These are complemented by early TV sets, plus memorabilia related to A-list broadcasting stars going back a century. Fittingly, another room offers a dressing-up box full of 1920s-style clothes for visitors to try on, and maybe practise a few Charleston dance poses in front of a mirror.

Other displays include vintage cameras, fossils, Alice's Vintage Kitchen, and the story of bathing machine proprietor Mary Wheatland – with an example of one of her machines. This room also pays homage to the British seaside tradition of Punch and Judy shows, including memorabilia for the 1963 film *The Punch and Judy Man*, starring legendary comedian Tony Hancock.

Recreated old shop displays cover diverse wares such as crafts and medicine, and a striking vintage poster adorns a section related to Bognor's tourism heyday. If you're particularly interested in the latter, there's a book on the town's long association with Butlin's holiday company in the excellent little museum shop.

Address 125 West Street, Bognor Regis, PO21 1XA, www.bognormuseum.org | Getting there 20-minute walk from Bognor Regis railway station | Hours Apr–Nov Tue–Sat 10am–4pm | Tip Admire the exterior of Sir Richard Hotham's grand 1790s mansion in nearby Hotham Park, where you can also enjoy a boating lake, adventure golf course, miniature railway and tropical gardens.

18 Elmer Rock Islands

Where striking sea defences star

Elmer Beach sits three miles east of Bognor Regis pier, and as elsewhere on this coast, faces a constant battle against erosion from a sea ceaselessly trying to shift its sand and shingle. It was the failure of traditional wooden groynes thrust out into the water to protect the beach that prompted the creation of the eight distinctive man-made rock islands lined up offshore today.

Some locals have affectionately nicknamed the feature the 'Rock Island Line', nodding to a classic 1920s US blues song. This found UK fame when singer Lonnie Donegan recorded a 1955 version, which swept into the British and American Top 10s as strongly as any wave! The track was also notable as the first debut record to be certified gold in the UK, as well as spurring the new musical movement known as skiffle.

In technical terms, the Elmer Rock Islands are 'offshore breakwaters', completed in 1993 in response to major flooding caused by storms in both 1984 and 1985. An even worse event struck in 1931, when a high tide coupled with south-easterly gales breached the then sea defences, and flooded a large part of a 1920s 'New City' resort that had been built here on the site of a former seaplane factory. This included a dance hall and tennis courts fashioned inside old aircraft hangars.

Each island is 70–125 metres long and around 15 metres wide, comprising man-made reefs made with 200,000 cubic metres of shingle and 100,000 tonnes of rock. As well as protecting the beach and creating a flat – and stable – expanse of sand at low tide, Elmer Rock Islands encourage a network of tidal pools which provide a great opportunity to pause from a coastal walk to explore for shells, shrimps and crabs. You're unlikely to find any eels hereabouts any more, however – even though the area is believed to owe its name to the Saxon description 'Ael-mere', combining the old English words for 'eel' and 'pool'.

Address Elmer Sands Estate, Bognor Regis, PO22 6AZ | **Getting there** Elmer Beach is a mile south of the A 259 between Bognor and Littlehampton; bus 600 runs to Elmer via Bognor Regis | **Hours** Accessible 24 hours | **Tip** Just behind the beach, The Elmer offers a seasonal Sussex-based pub menu plus six bedrooms (www.elmermiddleton.co.uk).

19__James Joyce Seaside Stay

How Bognor shaped a surreal literary masterpiece

Though James Joyce's strange trailblazing novel *Finnegans Wake* was spurred by the author's years amid the creative foment of inter-war Paris, key elements in its origin came from a summer break Joyce took with his wife Nora in Bognor Regis from 29 June to 3 August 1923. The link is recalled today by a blue plaque on what was once the Alexandra Guest House on Clarence Road – now a private home just off the seafront.

For starters, the holiday gave Joyce the name of his novel's central figure, Humphrey Chimpden Earwicker, along with associated fictional family ties. Literary detectives tracked down the link to a 1923 Bognor guidebook, which noted how tombstones at nearby Sidlesham Church provided a feast of curious names, 'striking examples being Earwicker, Glue, Gravy, Boniface, Anker, and Northeast'. Compare this to *Finnegans Wake*, where Joyce talks of his key character's odd surname, as well as 'such pivotal ancestors as the Glues, the Gravys, the Northeasts, the Ankers and the Earwickers of Sidlesham'.

Bognor is also the setting for a park scene when The Cad accosts Earwicker, when The Cad is described as a Dubliner who has moved to Sussex, settling in 'the southeast bluffs of the stranger stepshore'. In his notes on the novel, Joyce lists this scene as 'Sun evg Bognor (cad)'.

Joyce also wrote a comic sketch in Bognor about St Patrick, which tried out a pidgin English developed in *Finnegans Wake*. Joyce biographer Richard Ellmann also claims the squawking of gulls on Bognor beach inspired Joyce to write his famous seagull song 'Three Quarks for Muster Mark!', which literary archives date back to July 1923. The word 'quark' that Joyce created is now used for a key category of subatomic particle. Despite grumbles about the guest house, the Joyces enjoyed Bognor, as James revealed in a letter: 'Here I am and I like it very much.'

Address 6 Alexandra Terrace, Clarence Road, Bognor Regis, PO21 1LA | Getting there 15-minute walk from Bognor Regis railway station | Hours Accessible 24 hours | Tip Literature fans should also head for the Heygates Bookshop beside Bognor Regis railway station to browse thousands of secondhand books (www.heygatesbookshop.com).

20 Mad Hatter Table
An icon of Wonderland in parkland

Along with its boating pool, bandstand and charming miniature railway, Bognor's Hotham Park now hosts a growing cast of life-sized characters from *Alice In Wonderland*, strikingly rendered in wood. Arrivals so far include the Queen of Hearts, White Rabbit, Alice herself, plus the Mad Hatter at the head of a long table spread with giant playing cards.

The sculptures, by Sussex artist Simon Groves, were commissioned by the Hotham Park Heritage Trust, with the Alice in Wonderland theme chosen by local schoolchildren. Groves, meanwhile, discovered his passion for chainsaw carving after making giant wooden initials for his sister's wedding. His work now appears in locations across the region, including an evocative carving of a World War I soldier standing in Littlehampton's Caffyns Field.

The Mad Hatter sculpture has become a particular favourite for park visitors thanks to its substantial carved table, ringed by giant mushroom-shaped chairs that allow visitors to have their own tea party with one of the kookiest characters from a famously kooky book.

The Mad Hatter figure also has a particular resonance for Bognor – where wealthy 18th-century London hatmaker Sir Richard Hotham sought to transform a little seaside village into an elegant seaside resort to rival nearby Brighton. The phrase 'Mad as a hatter' also nods to his trade, believed to have risen from the shaking, mood swings and other mental issues some hatters suffered due to their nervous systems being poisoned by the mercury once commonly used in making headwear.

It took Groves 15 days to create the 8-foot by 2.5 foot Mad Hatter table, complete with clocks in each corner. Funds for the Wonderland sculptures have been raised from the annual Hotham Park Heritage Trust Country Fair held each August, with hopes that further sculptures will appear in the park over the coming years.

Address Hotham Park, Upper Bognor Road, Bognor Regis, PO21 1HW, www.grovessculpture.co.uk | Getting there Hotham Park is a 10-minute walk from Bognor Regis railway station | Hours Park open daily 6.30am–10pm | Tip Enjoy a tea party – plus excellent pizzas and much else – at Hotham Park Cafe, just a stone's throw from the Mad Hatter table.

21 Picturedrome
Memories of vintage entertainment history

With its octagonal lantern tower rising opposite the railway station, the Picturedrome has provided a striking landmark welcoming visitors to Bognor Regis since Victorian times. Now Grade II listed, the building opened in May 1886 as the Assembly Rooms, providing a venue for everything from stage shows, dancing and roller-skating to badminton and community functions.

By 1911, its name had changed to the Queens Hall – and the building had forged links to cinema through screenings showcasing the new art form of moving pictures. It's worth noting that many of the pioneering innovations in film-making were made in the 1890s and early 1900s, just along the south coast in Brighton and Hove. Sadly, there is no footage of the quirkiest aspect of the Picturedrome's early history. This saw boys pedalling a bicycle-type mechanism to turn a revolving light which shone from the octagonal tower to advertise the building's presence for miles around!

World War I saw the building become an army drill hall and barracks, but with the return of peace, entertainment returned too – and in 1919, the Picturedrome cinema was born. Over the next century, ownership changed many times, until the early 21st century brought talk of the building being converted into apartments. Thankfully, in 2010, Bognor Regis Town Council – supported by electors – rejected those plans, and instead bought the building for the town.

Though today visitors can watch films with all modern technology in place in terms of screen and sound, the Picturedrome still retains a host of characterful hints to its long history.

In granting Listed status, for example, English Heritage picked out special features, such as the coloured glass Picturedrome sign, the external projection room, vintage boxes flanking the 1911 proscenium, and the unusual survival of an early pay desk dating to 1919.

Address 51 Canada Grove, Bognor Regis, PO21 1DW, www.picturedromebognor.com |
Getting there Opposite Bognor Regis railway station | Hours Screenings begin at 10am,
and the cinema closes after the end of the last, at around 11pm | Tip Fans of vintage picture
houses can also head 15 miles east to The Dome cinema in the neighbouring seaside town of
Worthing, which began showing films back in 1911 (www.domecinema.co.uk).

22 Pink's Parlour

Ice cream beacon built on happy chance

If ice cream's your thing, who better to guide you than the President of the Ice Cream Alliance? Katy Alston's adventures in the cold stuff began by chance one chilly Christmas morning in 2001. That was when her husband Kevin surprised her with a very unexpected gift – a clapped out old ice cream van that was more scrap-heap challenge than vintage beauty! But, working alongside her daughter Georgia, Katy – now going under the name 'Mrs Whippy' – decided to put ice cream at the centre of her working life.

Beginning in 2013 with a single van, the business that became Pinks Vintage has gone from strength to strength, going from one decrepit old vehicle to two state-of-the-art machines nicknamed Terence and Patsy – plus a traditional British 'Pashley' tricycle called Rosey! A slew of awards followed, including Mobiler of the Year for Kate / Mrs Whippy at the 2015 Ice Cream Alliance Awards, while Georgia (aka 'Little Miss Whippy') scooped the Guido Morelli Rising Star Award at the National Ice Cream Competition in 2019.

Despite the success of their mobile trade, there was always a desire for a more permanent base – leading to the opening of Pink's Parlour just back from the Bognor Regis seafront in 2019. By way of pre-opening research, Katy and Georgia even went to Italy – not only to pick up ice cream-making insights, but also to get their serving counter handmade in quality traditional style.

Today, a regular stream of customers choose from a dazzling and colourful variety of flavours, from simple but beautifully made classics to more unusual offerings such as Guinness ice-cream or Pina Colada sorbet. The 'Unicorn' ice cream, meanwhile, seeks to combine candy floss with 'a taste of soft clouds'! Even better, you can watch 'Mrs Whippy' or one of her expert team create gelato in front of your eyes at the shop's very own Ice Cream Lab.

Address 18 Waterloo Square, Bognor Regis, PO21 1SU, www.pinksparlour.co.uk | Getting there 15-minute walk from Bognor Regis railway station | Hours Daily 11am–5pm | Tip To enjoy another quintessential British seaside experience, challenge yourself to an 18-hole round at Bognor Regis Crazy Golf, just 100 metres south of Pink's Parlour (www.facebook.com/bognorregisminigolf).

23 __ The White Tower

Dazzling home fashioned with divine inspiration

This remarkable modernist house was among the earliest works by an equally remarkable architect – John Cyril Hawes. Built in 1898 for Hawes and his two brothers when John was just 21, The White Tower kickstarted a career that combined creating buildings in the UK, Australia and The Bahamas, with a complementary life as a priest.

After graduating from Cambridge in 1897, Hawes began work on what he described as a 'curious looking building', designed to obtain sea views by looking over houses on the seaward side of the street. As Hawes wrote: 'Instead of a long spread out cottage I would stand it up on end – as a tower'.

The resulting gleaming edifice riffs on Arts and Crafts style, featuring four rooms atop each other, accessed by a side turret staircase with a viewing parapet on top of the building. At the rear, a two-storey wing contains larger rooms and a studio. The distinctive lintel over the front door bears a Latin inscription which, rather than alluding to some grand idea, simply translates as: 'John caused this house to be built as a triple home for Edward, Robert, and himself, in 1898'.

After being ordained as a priest in 1903, an 'act of God' set him on an international path in 1908 when a devastating hurricane destroyed all the churches on Long Island in The Bahamas – and perhaps the world's only architect priest went on to restore four of them. He also built a simple house for himself at the islands' highest point on Como Hill.

Hawes then lived in Western Australia from 1915–1939, building a host of religious buildings including St Francis Xavier Cathedral. This tie to Australia drew a group of pilgrims across the world to Bognor to visit The White Tower in 2018. Hawes, meanwhile, asked to be buried at Como Hill when he died in 1956, and it was there he was laid – with no coffin – in a 'little cave' that he had readied to be his final home.

Address 16 Aldwick Road, Bognor Regis, PO21 2LP, www.monsignorhawes.com/white-tower-bognor-regis | Getting there Train to Bognor Regis, then a 20-minute walk | Hours Exterior accessible 24 hours | Tip Architecture fans can book to stay in a nearby 1930s Art Deco house called Three Decks, built for a sea captain beside Elmer Beach a few miles east along the coast (www.cottages.com).

24 Almshouse Arcade

Vintage reminders of a rich shopping past

Chichester once boasted a host of little historic shopping arcades, but today only two survive: the Butter Market and Almshouse Arcade – a charming beacon of vintage retail in The Hornet. Until the 1970s, the site was home to Old Dears' Almshouses – not a cheeky reference to the elderly ladies of slender means that it housed, but a nod to local philanthropist Martha Dear, who left a legacy of £1,000 – equal to around £100,000 today – to fund the almshouses when she died in 1807. The building itself dates to 1802.

Among the mainly vintage-themed traders, Roxy's Box has attracted most attention for offering 'queer' style from local artists and alternative designers influenced by the LGBTQ+ scene. Owner Roxy proclaims a wish to be 'Andy Warhol meets Vivian Westwood!'. She aims to provide a place for people in Chichester who feel unrepresented and invisible. She wants people who may feel 'different' to visit Roxy's Box and feel welcome.

Meanwhile, retro fashion is the order of the day at Almshouse Vintage, including 1920s Flapper accessories and late-1940s outfits such as tailored jackets, lace and silk-trimmed tops, gorgeous beading and period hats, ranging from pillbox to fedora. By way of complement, LaylaLeigh Millinery sells striking 21st-century bespoke headwear – the kind of thing certain to draw admiring glances at events such as Goodwood Revival, the celebration of vintage motor racing staged every September at Goodwood House, just a few miles north of Chichester.

Nostalgia fans in playful mood can remind themselves of treasured childhood toys – Dinky cars, model trains, dolls – at Collector's Toys, while Collector's Corner, just next door, is likely to attract those interested in ceramics and coins. Time Machine Records, as the name suggests, celebrates vinyl records and pop/rock memorabilia going back to the swinging 60s.

Address 19 The Hornet, Chichester, PO19 7JL | Getting there 20-minute walk from Chichester railway station | Hours Mon 10am–4pm, Tue 9am–4pm, Wed–Fri 9am–5pm, Sat 9am–4.30pm | Tip Channel vintage passions further at two nearby outlets on The Hornet: rummage retro fashion from the 1920s–1970s at Beyond The Fringe, and admire the selection of 19th-century toys at Squirrel Antiques.

25 Beeding Toll House
Relocated embodiment of past travel

It's hard to choose just one of the 50-plus evocative rural buildings moved lock, stock and barrel from elsewhere to rise again amid South Downs vistas at the wonderful open-air Weald and Downland Living Museum. With buildings ranging from the 1300s to 1910 – furnished with vintage artefacts – this is like a unique village for time travellers.

Its interior speaks of humble cottage living, with basic furnishings around an unadorned fireplace, but the Beeding Toll House taps into radical shifts in how roads functioned. In medieval times, their upkeep was the responsibility of landowners, before Tudor authorities shifted the burden onto local parishes. With every householder having to contribute six days' work each year for road upkeep, this wasn't a welcome change.

In 1663, the first of what became a multitude of Turnpike Trusts was created. These placed barriers every few miles along highways, with toll collectors living alongside to raise the barriers on payment of a fee. The tariff board attached to the Beeding Toll House offers resonant details around past travel. It cost 4½ old pennies, for example, 'For every Horse, Mule, Ass or Other Beast (except Dogs)' pulling diverse wheeled vehicles with names such as Barouche, Curricle or Whiskey Taxed Cart Wagon. And this applied only if their wheels were less than 4.5 inches wide.

When built in 1807, the Beeding Toll House oversaw one of over 1,100 turnpikes covering the country. The system, however, was unable to cope with increasing traffic or competition from the railway, and the Beeding turnpike eventually closed in 1885 – the last public road in Sussex to levy a toll. The building lay abandoned by the road until literally falling victim to heavy traffic, when a lorry crashed into it in 1967! Dismantled by the Museum's first volunteer group in 1968, it was reborn at its present site in 1980.

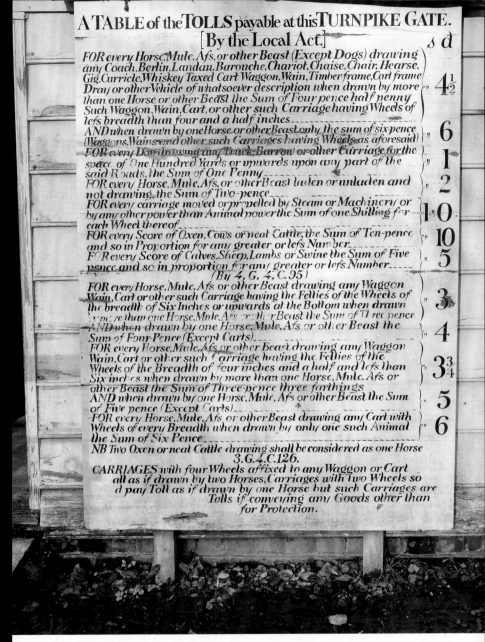

Address Town Lane, Singleton, PO18 0EU, www.wealddown.co.uk | Getting there By car via the A286 between Chichester and Midhurst; bus 60 from Chichester Cathedral to the Grooms Yard stop in Singleton, then a 5-minute walk | Hours Daily 10.30am–4pm | Tip The traditional 16th-century Partridge Inn offers not only a cosy place to enjoy local beer and food in Singleton village, but also highlights routes for diverse walks around the lovely surrounding countryside (www.thepartridgeinn.co.uk).

26 The Big Deal

Wow – is that a Banksy?

At first sight, this unusual street art work on North Pallant could be mistaken for a Banksy, in both style and use of stencils. But the signature, 'JPS', suggests that this artist is, unlike Banksy, happy to share his identity. Jamie Paul Scanlon painted the image of two girls swapping bank notes near Pallant House Gallery in 2015. Dark undertones abound on close inspection. The faces seem aged and wary rather than girlish, more like malevolent elves. The strange square box carried by one of them exudes a military air.

Scanlon's rainbow-coloured cat in nearby West Pallant has a companion piece called 'Caturday', depicted on a wall in Barcelona. Indeed, the JPS tag adorns walls across Europe, and the artist's work has also been exhibited at London's Tate Modern. Fans highlight Scanlon's wit – such as a depiction of Batman in his hometown Weston-super-Mare, accompanied by the words 'Painted On A Dark Knight'.

Scanlon credits Banksy as both an artistic influence and personal saviour. In the *Chichester Observer* in 2016, he revealed that 'Banksy inspired me, he saved my life'. This followed a 12-year period during which Scanlon suffered homelessness, drink and drug abuse, and friends lost to murder. It was when the artist visited a Banksy show in Bristol that he was inspired to take up street art of his own – and this has helped turn his life around.

Elsewhere in Chichester, street art fans can find work by other noted creatives in the field such as Stik, Thierry Noir and Roa. A four-metre-high work *King of Cats* by Belgium's Joachim is a showstopper on the same wall as JPS's *The Big Deal*. But Scanlon's personal story is as inspiring as his art. Speaking to Streetart360.net Scanlon said: 'I chose to not hide my real identity to let people know that it is possible to beat addiction and turn your life around if you are prepared to put in the effort.'

Address North Pallant, Chichester, PO19 1TJ | Getting there 10-minute walk from Chichester railway station; many buses to the Market Cross | Hours Unrestricted | Tip Keep tabs on JPS's latest work via his Instagram site: @jps_artist

27 Bishop's Palace Garden
A lush medieval oasis

Cradled between the south side of Chichester's Roman city walls and the soaring Cathedral lies the Eden-like 14-acre expanse of the Bishop's Palace Gardens. The Bishop's Palace itself – on the north side of the gardens – dates to the 12th century, built for Bishop Seffrid II following a fire that devastated both Cathedral and town in 1187. The gardens, however, pre-date the present Palace, having been established in the late 1140s.

Despite this great age, the Garden is constantly refreshed with new plantings, and additions such as water features, new seating and a pergola walk, alongside improved access and the creation of particular wildlife-friendly spaces. In tune with the growing urban agriculture movement, meanwhile, a large area is now being used by the local charity Grow Chichester for producing fruit and vegetables. They also offer regular gardening sessions for the public throughout the year.

There is a host of notable trees for arboreal fans to seek out in the Garden. Among a gaggle of palm trees by the entrance off Canon Lane is a rare UK example of a Chusan palm – a tropical variety that has thrived here since its 2007 planting, thanks to the protective flanking of ancient brick walls. Out in the wider green expanse, meanwhile, is a 250-year-old Holm Oak which boasts the widest trunk in Sussex.

There is also a Wollemi Pine, a fascinating variety discovered in Australia in 1994. Related to the monkey puzzle tree, its bark is often compared to bubbly chocolate! Fewer than 100 examples have been found, which prompted the sending of cuttings around the world to provide the best chance of its survival as a species. The Chichester example was planted in 2008. The Garden also hosts a Giant Sequoia – nicknamed 'Big Tree' as the largest seed plant in the world. With a height of 27 metres, this is by far the tallest tree in central Chichester.

Address Canon Lane, Chichester, PO19 1PY | **Getting there** 10-minute walk from Chichester railway station | **Hours** Daily 8am–dusk | **Tip** The Garden hosts regular public events, including Tree Trail walks with specialist wardens, as well as performances from local community choirs during the Festival of Chichester held every June and July.

28__Boxgrove Priory
Ancient edifice with poignant American link

Few people whizzing past on the nearby A 27 seem aware of the beacon of history – from medieval to World War II – just a few hundred metres off the highway, including the evocative ruins of a Benedictine priory founded around 1107 for a select group of just three monks. Following the dissolution of the monasteries by Henry VIII in 1536, what we see today is the remains of the guest house, still reaching to its full two-storey height.

Beside the ruins stands the old priory church, though the original 12th-century edifice morphed into the 16th-century parish Church of St Mary and St Blaise. While its interior style nods to both Norman (Romanesque) and Early English (Gothic) architecture, it's the gorgeous painted ceiling that leaps out. Created by local artist Lambert Barnard, it was commissioned by the 9th Lord de la Warr, keen to adorn the nave with the arms and badges of his own and his wife's families, entwined with flowers and foliage. Alas, His Lordship didn't get much chance to enjoy the result, as he was forced by the Crown to swap the church and priory for an estate in Hampshire in 1538.

Wander along the nave to discover one of the most unusual stained glass windows in Britain, depicting a Hurricane fighter plane along with a US Stars and Stripes flag, with a dedication to one William Fiske – a Chicago-born pilot who became the first American serviceman to die in World War II. Flying out of nearby RAF Tangmere, he was killed in the skies over Sussex during the Battle of Britain on 17 August 1940.

Fiske's funeral took place here three days later, though it wasn't until 2008 that the stained glass window was created by Mel Howse, commissioned by the 601 Squadron Old Comrade's Association. Fiske's grave in the churchyard draws American visitors to lay flowers and mementoes by a headstone with the simple but moving inscription, *He died for England.*

Address The Street, Boxgrove, Chichester, PO18 0EE, www.boxgrovepriory.co.uk | **Getting there** By car, half a mile off the A27, turning north at the Tangmere roundabout; bus 55 runs to Boxgrove, taking around 25 minutes | **Hours** Priory ruins open daily; church open after Mass every day until dusk; Mass held Mon, Tue, Thu, Sat 10am, Wed & Fri noon, Sun 8.30am and 10.30am | **Tip** Just half a mile north of the Priory, the Anglesey Arms is a thoughtfully renovated historic gastropub beside the A285, named after a hero of the Battle of Waterloo: Halnaker, Chichester PO18 0NQ (www.theangleseyarms.com).

29_ Candida Stevens Gallery

Contemporary art in an old flour mill

Candida Stevens is proof that not all major contemporary art dealers are born in big cities – though the gallery founded in Chichester in 2013 does now also have an outpost in London, so they don't
feel left out. Their Chichester HQ occupies a simple ground floor
space in a former 19th-century flour mill, where it showcases work
in different media by some of the most interesting artists working
in Britain today.

Speaking at the 2018 Affordable Art Fair, Candida Stevens
explained how the gallery came to be founded on the back of an
exhibition called Good Figures, which she took from the Mall Galleries in London to the Jerwood Gridshell space at the Weald and
Downland Living Museum. The hugely positive reception that followed this example of a commercial West Sussex showcase for high
quality contemporary British artists spurred her to consider setting
up a gallery on a permanent basis. 'And there just happened to be the
perfect space in an old warehouse in Chichester ready for conversion.
We bravely just went for it.'

One example of the artists championed by the gallery is Alice
Kettle, best known for large-scale works bringing together textiles and embroidery to explore social and political topics. Kettle's
2019 exhibition at Candida Stevens, for example, involved refugees
the artist encountered during her Thread Bearing Witness project.
Works began with drawings, which were then scanned and printed
on to fabric, before being intricately embroidered. These collaborative
stitched works were made with a mix of now UK-based refugees from
Syria, Iran, Pakistan and Uganda, as well as artisans based in Pakistan.

Other standouts in the gallery roster are the pop culture-influ-
enced paintings by poet-turned-artist Anthony Stevens, Suzanne
Knight's multi-media reflections on female domesticity, and Cecilia
Charleston's giant abstract embroideries.

Address 12 Northgate, Chichester, PO19 1BA, www.candidastevens.com | **Getting there** 20-minute walk from Chichester railway station | **Hours** Wed–Fri 10am–5pm, Sat 11am–2pm | **Tip** If you feel inspired to get creative yourself, The Works offers a wide range of art materials just a few hundred metres away.

30 Cathedral Grotesques

Locals immortalised affectionately in stone

Many will know the term 'gargoyle' for a scary figure cast in stone adorning the walls of ancient churches. These are more correctly called grotesques, with gargoyles referring to those serving a specific purpose as artfully disguised drainpipes to channel rainwater away from the church roof.

In ancient times, depicting monsters and demons in these figures served as a reminder to illiterate congregations of the imagined perils of the world from which the Church offered protection. For centuries, however, stonemasons also traditionally included their own likeness carved in stone somewhere on the building as an eternal reminder of their work. So when restoration was carried out on the south side of the Cathedral in the 1930s, masons kept up that tradition by creating waterspouts featuring wonderfully distinctive likenesses of nearly a dozen real-life church employees of the time.

Those immortalised in stone ranged from grand figures such as Chichester's then Bishop Langton and Archdeacon Ven Hoskyns, to humbler folk such as builder Cecil Norman and Jack Parsons, foreman of the restoration team. Others whose faces now peer out from the Cathedral wall include 1930s organist Dr Harvey Grace, and the then church treasurer, Right Reverend Hordern. Without photographs of these individuals from the time, however, precisely identifying which gargoyle refers to whom isn't easy!

Terms such as gargoyle and grotesque could sometimes be deemed inappropriate, though, when mentioning the likenesses of the late Queen Elizabeth II and Prince Philip above the entrance to Chichester Cathedral; a more respectful term is corbels. There are corbels of illustrious 1930s figures inside the church, including King George V, flanked by two key parliamentarians of the day, placed to reflect their political positions: Ramsay MacDonald to the left, and Stanley Baldwin to the right.

Address Chichester Cathedral, Chichester, PO19 1PX, www.chichestercathedral.org.uk |
Getting there 10-minute walk from Chichester railway station | Hours Accessible
24 hours | Tip Alongside browsing for books, go upstairs at Waterstones across the road
from the Cathedral to see a characterful space that was once a dance hall!

31 Cawley Almshouses

Resonant reminder of past social attitudes

The history of this lovely building sheds light not just on one of the most turbulent times in the town's history, but also on past attitudes to social welfare. Cawley Almshouses were founded here in 1625 by William Cawley, son of a wealthy local brewer. Initially called St Bartholomew's Hospital, its purpose was for the 'residence and maintenance of 12 decayed tradesmen of Chichester'. That charitable ethos seems to have lessened after Cawley's death in 1667, as a 1681 record shows the Almshouses morphed into a Workhouse.

These were harsh places, where poor people seeking support were worked hard in exchange for help. Local police could also detain – and work – the children of poor parents. Punishments for those who broke the rules or failed to 'preserve good Harmony' included starvation or wearing notices proclaiming things such as 'Infamous Lyar'. Misbehaviour could also earn imprisonment in the stocks – or receiving 30 lashes on the bare back with a 'Catt and nine tails'.

Cawley's own life had its share of troubles. As the MP for Chichester, in August 1642 he declared the town for the Parliamentary side in the English Civil War between Parliament and Charles I, but then had to flee to Portsmouth when Royalists seized the town. He returned when Parliamentary forces recaptured Chichester after a siege, in which Cawley's Almshouses provided a vantage point to direct cannon fire.

Cawley was one of the people who signed Charles I's death warrant, so when the monarchy was restored under Charles II he had to flee again – first to Belgium and then to Vevey in Switzerland, where he died. Cawley had always wished to be buried in the almshouse chapel back in Chichester, however – and the 19th-century discovery of a lead case with a male skeleton in a vault under the floor suggests that Cawley's body may indeed have been secretly smuggled home.

Address 972 Broyle Road, Chichester, PO19 6BY | Getting there 30-minute walk from Chichester railway station | Hours Exterior accessible 24 hours | Tip A 17th-century portrait believed to be of William Cawley can be seen at the Chichester Council building on North Street (www.artuk.org/discover/artworks).

32 Cedar of Lebanon
Veteran tree in a 1960s setting

Goodwood has been the seat of the Dukes of Richmond, Lennox, Gordon & Aubigny since the late 17th century. The house has a curious layout, like a truncated star, or an unfinished hexagon, and reflects a complex story of changing architectural tastes – and dry rot.

It started as a Jacobean hunting lodge, but changed significantly during the 18th century, when it received a Classical makeover and new wings by the architects Roger Morris, Matthew Brettingham and eventually James Wyatt. It now sports a three-sided façade, dominated by Wyatt's copper-domed turrets, but walk to the back of the house and you may be surprised by the somewhat incongruous combination of old and modern features, both architectural and natural, including a monumental cedar tree. These tell us more about the history of the house and estate.

Wyatt added a north wing in the 1770s to balance a Palladian-style south wing built in 1750. In the 1960s, the north wing was found to be riddled with dry rot, and a decision was made to tear it down – apart from one room. An external colonnade and modern kitchens were created at the same time, in a minimalist, almost Brutalist style typical of the late 1960s.

At the end of the colonnade is a circular concrete feature behind which the very tall cedar towers. This is one of around 2,000 Cedars of Lebanon planted from the 1740s onward, by the tree-loving second Duke. He had proposed 'making a Mount Lebanon upon a very high hill' at Goodwood.

Some of the surviving cedars count among the finest and most monumental trees in the country. This one isn't the largest on the estate: you'll find another with a girth of nearly 10 metres on the south side of the cricket field. However, the ancient tree, in conjunction with the minimalist 1960s structures, creates an almost Zen-like scene. A great place to rest on your visit to Goodwood.

Address Goodwood House, Chichester, PO18 0PX, +44 (0)1243 755055, www.goodwood.com/visit-eat-stay/goodwood-house | Getting there Goodwood is located just outside Chichester, a 12-minute taxi ride from Chichester station; by car via the A27 and A285 | Hours Opening times vary; for information, contact the ticket office | Tip The surviving part of the Wyatt's north wing, the Tapestry Drawing Room, features a charming set of 18th-century Gobelins tapestries, showing scenes from the story of Don Quixote.

33 Chalk Stone Trail

Artist raises questions of time and place

In the summer of 2002, 13 large balls of pure chalk appeared in the West Sussex countryside, like a string of beads, between West Dean College and the village of Cocking. Chalk is one of the main geological features of Sussex, and its soft, porous nature gives the Sussex Downs their distinctive, undulating, soft-edged appearance. Seeing chalk boulders, ridges, paths and cliffs comes as no surprise in this county, but these chalk balls were clearly some kind of human intervention in the landscape, dug out, shaped and placed in a certain order and pattern by human hands. They were indeed sculptures, excavated and carved from a nearby quarry by the Scottish artist Andy Goldsworthy, for a collaborative project with Chichester's Pallant House Gallery. The aim was to celebrate the Sussex landscape.

Goldsworthy placed the stones along a five-mile walking route through the Downs, creating a path that leads over hills and into valleys, through open fields and dense woodland, crossing the South Downs Way. Walking the trail will take around 2.5 hours, during which you may feel like a treasure hunter, while trying to distinguish art from nature, and white from green.

Goldsworthy's art is conceptual, immersive and emotional, engaging us both physically and mentally. Using only natural materials, he incorporates decay, change and disappearance into his work. A few years earlier, he had placed large frozen snowballs in London, which gradually melted. In 2002 the stones were gleaming white and large (around two metres in diameter), but more than 20 years later, you wonder how much of them is still left, and how their colour and texture have changed. Have some dissolved completely, or been usurped by woodland vegetation? How do things, people, places change over time? Search for these chalky markers in the landscape, and you might find some answers.

Address Start at West Dean Garden: PO18 0RX; download the brochure for the complete trail: www.walkandcycle.co.uk/sussex/Trails/50-99/SUSSTR0088.pdf | Getting there Train to Chichester, then bus 60 to either Cocking Hill or West Dean Gardens; by car via the A286 | Hours Trail always open but check opening times for West Dean Gardens if starting there | Tip Cocking's delightful ancient church, St Catherine of Siena, was built around 1080 by the Normans, although its Saxon font suggests that a much older wooden church was there before; look out for some remains of 13th-century wall paintings.

34_Charles Crocker Plaque

Faded glory in the story of a shoemaker poet

An unobtrusive plaque by the entrance of Kim's Bookshop on South Street recognises not just the former home of a once celebrated poet, but also the fickleness of fame. In his 19th-century heyday, Charles Crocker was considered one of Britain's best poets, with one poem hailed as perhaps 'the finest… in the English language'. Yet today, he is all but forgotten.

Crocker rose from humble roots. Born in Chichester of poor parents, Charles left school at the age of 11 to be apprenticed to a local shoemaker – an occupation he continued until he was 47. But alongside his work tending the soles of Chichester's citizens, Crocker also delved into his soul to write poetry celebrating the surrounding Sussex landscape. Encouraged by local doctor John Forbes, Crocker sent some poems to a Brighton paper, and, encouraged by the response, undertook some Georgian crowdfunding to raise money to publish a collection. Entitled *Kingley Vale and other Poems*, it came out to great acclaim in 1830, and included a sonnet 'To The British Oak' which Poet Laureate Robert Southey cited as among the best English had to offer.

By the mid 1840s, Crocker was earning enough from poetry to give up shoemaking for good – as well as another job he had taken in the bookselling department of his poetry publisher. In 1845, he became sexton of Chichester Cathedral and, later, bishop's verger.

Crocker devoted as much attention to the wonders of the Cathedral as to his poetry, leading him to publish an 1848 handbook on the building entitled *A Visit to Chichester Cathedral* – the first ever guide to the Cathedral. Crocker delighted in showing visitors around, and sharing stories of the shrines and ornaments in this ancient place of worship. The sudden collapse of the cathedral spire in 1861 so distressed Crocker that it was said to have contributed to his untimely death later that year.

Address 28 South Street, Chichester, PO19 1EL | **Getting there** 10-minute walk from Chichester railway station | **Hours** Accessible 24 hours | **Tip** Follow in the footsteps of Charles Crocker by taking one of the daily tours offered at Chichester Cathedral (www.chichestercathedral.org.uk/visiting-us/tours).

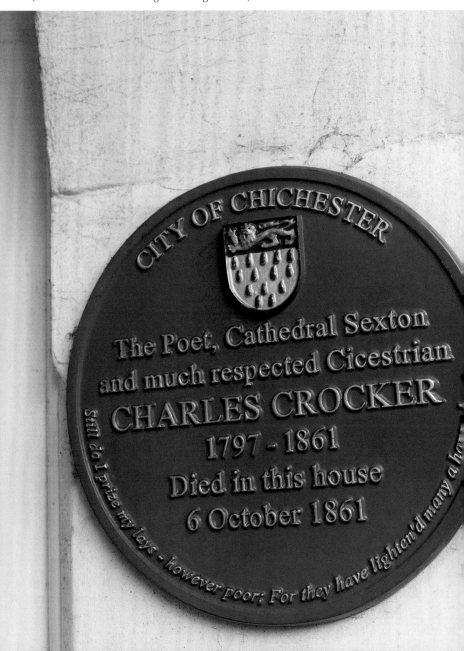

35 Chichester Lakes

Sussex's secret Lake District

This watery wonderland just outside Chichester features 11 lakes of varying sizes, set in over 150 acres of countryside, ringed with places to stay and complemented by little trails. Nine of the lakes are fishing spots (licence required), while Ivy Lake is a water sport beacon, and New Lake a nature reserve. The Lakeside Holiday Park offers a chance to sleep over in luxury lodges set beside the water, complemented by an entertainment and leisure venue, plus the option for al fresco dining on a wide wooden lakeside deck. The lakes range in size from 1.5-acre pools all the way up to 52 acres. They were excavated in the late 1930s and 1940s, then stocked with fish. Each named lake has been fashioned in terms of layout, depth and types of fish, to provide different challenges to anglers of all standards.

In terms of ecology, West Lake is perhaps the most diverse. Large and shallow, weedy in places, it is home to a superb array of fish species, including carp weighing up to 20kg, pike (up to 15kg) and tench (up to 5kg). Those in the know suggest fishing for carp from the north bank, while some of the best pike landed here have been caught from the bay by the bridle path that rings the lake. Other species include sizeable bream, rudd, roach and perch. It's also possible to catch eels in all of the lakes. At the other end of the scale, the Nunnery is a tranquil 1.5-acre elongated pool that's home to carp weighing up to 15kg, as well as other species. An ample fringing of weeds provides plentiful bank-side cover for fish which, though it brings them close in to shore, also increases the challenge of catching them!

Licences are available from 24-hour tickets up to season tickets covering months. Note that pike fishing is allowed only between November and February – and anyone found not returning fish to the water can face prosecution.

Address Vinnetrow Road, Chichester, PO20 1QH, www.parkholidays.com/our-parks/sussex/chichester-lakeside | **Getting there** By car via the A27, take the Pagham exit at the Bognor roundabout just outside Chichester; bus 51 runs to the stop for Chichester Free School, which is across the road from The Nunnery and Ivy Lake | **Hours** Accessible 24 hours | **Tip** The Chichester Waterski Club offers a Visitor Day Pass for anyone looking for an exciting way to get out on the water: www.chichesterwaterski.club.

36__Chichester Ship Canal

Watery thread that finally found a purpose

Visitors arriving by train into Chichester overwhelmingly head up South Street toward the bustle of the town centre. But go in the opposite direction, and within 200 metres you'll find the boat-dotted basin of the historic Chichester Ship Canal, which runs four miles south to join the sea at Birdham Pool.

Given Chichester's past pre-eminence, plans to link the town to the sea date back to an Act of Parliament passed in 1585. But just to prove that even in the old days, politicians promised things they didn't deliver, nothing happened. In fact, despite further schemes being proposed, it wasn't until 1819 that a new Act was passed that saw real work done. The canal finally opened in 1822, for boats up to 100 tons – only two and a half centuries late.

Originally intended as part of a much longer canal linking London to Portsmouth that never materialised, by the 1840s the Chichester Canal had fallen into a ruinous state, choked with vegetation and with bridges and locks in disrepair. Though the Corporation of Chichester tried in the 1890s to restore the canal, their efforts failed to spark a return of traffic. The last commercial cargo was a load of shingle carried from Birdham in 1906 – though the canal wasn't formally closed to commercial traffic until 1928.

Now run by the Chichester Ship Canal Trust charity, it's a hive of pleasurable activity: rowing and canoeing, nature rambles, fishing and cycling. Two canal boats run regular scenic trips – including fish-and-chip and afternoon tea cruises – along the two-mile section between the Basin and Donnington, offering a glimpse of bird life including herons, kingfishers, coots, mallards, sandpipers and flycatchers. You can also walk for two miles along the towpath to Hunston Bridge to look back towards Chichester Cathedral, and experience a glorious view painted by the great British painter J. M. W. Turner in 1828.

Address Canal Basin, Canal Wharf, Chichester, PO19 8DT, www.chichestercanal.org.uk | Getting there The Basin is a 5-minute walk from Chichester railway station; bus 51 runs every 15 minutes from Chichester bus station to Hunston; bus 52 and 53 to Chichester Marina at Birdham Pool | Hours Accessible 24 hours | Tip There is a Heritage Centre exploring the Canal's history in a 19th-century stable block at the Basin, along with a café where you can taste or buy local products, including honey from nearby Fishbourne.

37 Corn Exchange

From corn to popcorn in classic style

So why is there what seems to be a Classical Greek temple standing proudly along one of Chichester's busiest shopping streets? Let's hear it for the power of agricultural trade! The Grade II-listed Corn Exchange was completed in 1833, financed by 70 local corn merchants, each contributing up to £250 (around £37,000 in today's money). Taking cues from the Greek Revivalist style, its six soaring Doric columns form what Classical architecture fans would recognise as a noble hexastyle portico. But despite its grand façade, flaws in the original construction required a major rebuild in 1836 after the roof was found to be so unsafe that the whole building was deemed in danger of collapse.

The building began a new life as an entertainment venue when the Chichester Minstrels performed here in 1884. Its major shift in use, however, came when one Maggie Morton brought an early cinematograph here on Boxing Day, 1896, to introduce local folk to the new-fangled invention of moving pictures. The *Chichester Observer* described it as 'the greatest sensation and most wonderful invention of the age', despite Morton's programme consisting of films no more than a minute long, and including one entitled *Gardeners burning weeds*!

In 1910, the building was taken over by Joseph Poole, and – as Poole's Picture Palace – became Chichester's first full-time cinema. The programmes improved too, including locally shot films of events such as the Bosham Regatta and cricket at nearby Priory Park. In 1929, the cinema – renamed The Exchange – was the first in West Sussex to show talking pictures. From the 1960s, however, cinema audiences began to fall as TV gained popularity. The Exchange finally closed as a cinema in 1980, bowing out with a screening of Star Wars film *The Empire Strikes Back*. Today, it's once again a place of trade – though now it sells clothes not corn.

Address East Street, Chichester, PO19 1HD | Getting there 15-minute walk from Chichester railway station | Hours Accessible 24 hours | Tip Tap into the retro vibe of the Corn Exchange's cinematic heyday among vintage fashion and memorabilia in the nearby Almshouse Arcade (www.almshousevintage.co.uk).

38 Dodo House

Gallery gateway reflecting natural history

Misunderstandings surround the bird statues topping gateposts at the entrance to Chichester's acclaimed Pallant House gallery. A common misconception is that they are meant to depict ostriches, but the 18th-century stonemason who made them had no idea what an ostrich looked like, so produced birds that gave the gallery its jokey local nickname 'The Dodo House'.

Like many urban myths, fact and fiction mix. It's true that Pallant House was built in 1712 as a grand home for wine merchant Henry Peckham, whose coat of arms included ostriches. It made sense, then, to feature these exotic birds by his front door.

The reason a giant flightless African bird was a thing for English family crests goes back to Roman times. While 1st-century-A.D. naturalist Pliny the Elder described ostriches based on sightings in Rome's African outposts, he also propagated the notion that they 'have the marvellous property of being able to digest every substance without distinction'. This strange idea sprang from the fact that, because ostriches lack teeth, they are known to swallow hard objects such as stones, which help the grinding of food in the gizzard. By medieval times, however, ostriches were being depicted in European art eating things such as iron, and had in turn become symbols of toughness and endurance, leading to them becoming part of the iconography of family crests.

Rather than mistaking the appearance of ostriches, the Pallant House statues reflect a more practical concern. An ostrich's large body on spindly legs was an inherently unstable sculptural form, while the long neck would have been a decapitation accident waiting to happen. The stonemason therefore had to make practical adjustments, including shortening legs and neck. Sure, the results may look more dodo than ostrich – but they have nonetheless proven tough enough to endure for centuries.

Address 9 North Pallant, Chichester, PO19 1TJ | Getting there 10-minute walk from Chichester railway station | Hours Sculptures accessible 24 hours; Pallant House gallery Tue–Sun 10am–5pm | Tip For a real-life thrill involving living birds, watch out for peregrine falcons that nest among the spires of nearby Chichester Cathedral each year from March to August. The Cathedral also offers a virtual live stream of the birds: chichestercathedral.org.uk/chichester-peregrines.

39 Dolphin Hotel

A former inn touched by politics and tragedy

The history of this landmark one-time inn on West Street dates back to the 17th century, though over the ensuing centuries it enjoyed a complex relationship with an adjacent inn called the Anchor, first mentioned in 1719. The two merged in 1910 to become the Dolphin and Anchor, which closed as a hotel in 1996 – though a bar with the same name beckons at ground level.

The building still bears striking golden dolphin and anchor emblems on its parapets, and was central to Chichester life for over two centuries, as well as being a key posting-house (an inn where horses were also kept) on the busy route to London. Records for the Dolphin start in the mid 1600s, when the building was recorded as having an impressive 23 hearths (fireplaces) – the same as the grand Bishop's Palace, a stone's throw away behind the Cathedral.

Stories of past tragedies cling to the building. One concerns the inn's carriage driver, Reuban Benham – great grandfather of author H. G. Wells – who died one stormy night after mistakenly driving a postal chaise off a quay. Charles Triggs, meanwhile, dropped dead at his own welcome party, just hours after taking over as the Dolphin's new landlord in 1813. The Dolphin has also seen differing forms of combat – most curiously, an 1830s bare-knuckle fight that pitted acclaimed poet and novelist George Meredith against Sussex County cricketer H. M. Hyndman, with Meredith winning what was described as a 'rough and tumble' contest.

The same description applied for a long time to local politics, with Chichester seeing bitter divisions from the 1640s during the Civil War into the 18th century. This was manifest when the Dolphin became the local base for the Whigs (akin to today's Liberal Democrats), while the neighbouring Anchor was the local HQ of the Tory party. A combination of proximity and alcohol meant political disputes often turned riotous.

DOLPHIN HOTEL

Address 9 West Street, Chichester, PO19 1QD | Getting there 15-minute walk from Chichester railway station | Hours Dolphin and Anchor bar open daily 8am–midnight | Tip For a characterful place to sup beer today, head for the Crafty Bishop ale house tucked down a lane near the Fountain pub (www.craftybishop.com).

40__ The Druid

Mistaken ID – plus secret links to a famous poet

This fine statue has been a feature of Priory Park's north-west corner since 1873. Its Chichester life, though, dates back to 1776, when it was first erected next to a water fountain in South Street. This was followed by several years in storage under the Sailors' Chapel in Chichester Cathedral, before being moved to the park. The identity of its sculptor remains a mystery – as was the identity of the figure for many years. Moses was one name in the frame, while others claimed it was Neptune. Research now points to it simply being a generalised image of a 'Druid'.

A key part of that ID was a cultish trend that sprang up around the time of the statue's creation. The period saw the appearance of secretive groups calling themselves Druids, inspired by those magical figures' links to the world of the ancient Britons. Their resonant spirituality inspired poets like William Blake – and Blake himself was believed to have joined an Ancient Order of Druids founded at the King's Arms tavern on the same London street (Poland Street) where the poet took up residence in 1790.

The Druid statue is also notable for being one of the most striking early examples of a revolutionary form of artificial material called Coade stone, invented in the 1760s. This took its name from Eleanor Coade, who created this amazing form of ceramic stoneware. It was initially called Lythodipyra, before being given her name. Both easily moulded and durable, Coade stone sparked a craze of creation in Georgian Britain, with more than 650 works appearing around the country to meet demand for neo-Classical ornamentation.

Its durability didn't, however, stop vandals breaking off the Druid's right arm in 2017. Though now repaired, some call for the statue to be moved inside the adjacent Guildhall – which would provide a reconnection with Blake, who was (unsuccessfully) tried there for sedition in 1804.

Address Priory Park, Chichester, PO19 1NS | **Getting there** 25-minute walk from Chichester railway station | **Hours** Accessible 24 hours | **Tip** See other examples of Coade Stone ornamentation around Chichester, including the crest on the Butter Market on North Street, plus the so-called Mercury Medallion adorning the façade of 31–32 East Street.

41 Edes House

Once nameless then misnamed architectural jewel

This red brick and Portland stone architectural beauty was built in 1696 for merchant John Edes, and has been described as the first new build of the Baroque period in England. Edes' worked as a maltster – preparing malt for brewing by germinating barley grains and then stopping the process with heat when certain changes had taken place in the grain. Sadly, John died before the building was completed, and it was his widow, Hannah, who took over supervision and completion of the construction.

Though Edes' initials – J. H. E. – are carved above the main entrance, the house itself remained nameless until 1841, when it was described as Westgate House in the will of later owner Elizabeth Penfold. It retained that name until 1905 when it was renamed West Street House. To add to the name-change carousel, for much of the 20th century the house was also commonly referred to as Wren House, due to claims that legendary architect Sir Christopher Wren had been involved in its construction. But this theory was cast aside in 1967, mainly because Wren would have been rather more occupied with rebuilding London's St Paul's Cathedral at the time. The house then acquired its current name.

The house originally boasted add-ons such as stables and outhouses, plus three acres of meadow. The 17th-century sundial remains in the garden, though its gnomon – the raised element that creates a shadow – was mysteriously relocated to a rose bed by the town's County Hall.

Edes House today provides a glorious wedding venue, but regular tours provide a chance for anyone to see its gorgeous interior. Each room channels its own unique period style, from Georgian onward. One highlight is the ravishing Arts & Crafts 'BBB' tiles in the Foyer, designed by William De Morgan for the firm Barnard, Bishop and Barnard around 1907, when the house was owned by noted artist Walter Ernest Tower.

Address 27 West Street, Chichester, PO19 1RQ, +44 (0) 1243 777265, edes.house@westsussex.gov.uk | Getting there 25-minute walk from Chichester railway station | Hours Public access Mon–Fri by appointment only, or via regular 90-minute guided tours every two months, Sun 11am; private tours also available, with the option of lunch or afternoon tea in the grand dining room | Tip Search out antique tiles for yourself at Chichester Architectural Salvage, located just off the A27 about two miles east of Chichester (www.architecturalsalvagesussex.co.uk).

42 — Egyptian Room at Goodwood

Dining in style with crocodiles

Charles Lennox (1735-1806), the 3rd Duke of Richmond, was a keen art collector and loved to entertain. In 1791, his London townhouse burnt down, and a new home had to be found for the salvaged art collection – so he decided to add two new wings to his country estate, Goodwood House, a few years later. For this, he hired the famous architect James Wyatt, also responsible for Goodwood's distinctive round towers with cupolas, and the opulent Regency interiors.

Wyatt's work included one of the most unusual rooms in any British country house, the so-called Egyptian Dining Room. Created between 1802 and 1806, it is decorated entirely in an Egyptian-inspired style, from gilded sphinxes and winged scarabs, and pylon-like door frames to bronze crocodiles on the backs of the dining chairs. The walls are covered in honey-coloured scagliola imitating marble. None of the decorations were actually Egyptian, except for a real mummy that dominated the far end of the room.

The Egyptian style was hugely popular in Western Europe at the time, fuelled by archaeological excavations and Napoleon's presence in Egypt. This room is one of the earliest examples of an interior inspired by ancient Egypt. Many of the motifs were lifted from Vivant Denon's magnificent illustrated book *Voyage dans la basse et la haute Egypte* (1802).

The Egyptian scheme wasn't always loved, in the early 20th century, the room was dismantled, and the sumptuous scagliola walls overpainted with a neo-Georgian scheme. In the 1990s, the complete refurbishment of Goodwood's Regency state rooms began, and the dining room was restored to its original splendour. Some replicas had to be made, modelled on similar objects in the Royal Pavilion in Brighton. The Egyptian mummy was not reinstated, though.

Address Goodwood House, Chichester, PO18 0PX, +44 (0)1243 755055, www.goodwood.com/visit-eat-stay/goodwood-house | Getting there Goodwood is located just outside Chichester, a 12-minute taxi ride from Chichester station; by car via the A 27 and A 285 | Hours Opening times vary; for information, contact the ticket office | Tip If you're wondering what kind of plates you'd have been eating from in the Egyptian Dining Room, go to the Card Room in one of the towers. There you'll see a spectacular display of 18th-century Sèvres porcelain, collected and commissioned by the third Duke; note the exceptionally large teapot!

43 Elisabeth Frink's Horse
A modern sculpture with an ancient spirit

Near the steps leading to the Richmond Pavilion at Goodwood Racecourse stands a life-sized sculpture of a horse, facing over the Sussex countryside. Cast in bronze, it's developed a blueish-green patina, and is realistically rendered, poised and elegant. At first glance, it might not be immediately obvious what's so special about it. But this is the work of Elisabeth Frink (1930–1993), the first woman sculptor to become a full Royal Academician – in 1979, the year before she made this horse.

Frink also very nearly became the first female President of the Royal Academy, but turned down the honour. Her work is at the heart of British mid 20th-century Modernism, though she is still lesser known than contemporaries, such as Barbara Hepworth or Henry Moore. Her work is edgy, hard, surreal, and at times disturbing. We can perhaps think of her as having translated the Brutalism of post-war architecture into sculpture. Many of her pieces are semi-abstract, and she took her inspiration from early Greek art, medieval sculpture, and – most importantly – animals.

Frink depicted horses from early in her artistic career, first in 1950s drawings with strong references to the Horsemen of the Apocalypse. Growing up during and in the aftermath of World War II, Frink was acutely aware of its horrors. She developed a keen interest in the psychological and physical nature of humanity, and how humans relate to animals. No doubt the idea of warhorses played a part in her sculptures, but for Frink, they also had much to do with the ancient spirit and symbolism of the horse, and its evolution in relation to humans.

For the Earl of March, who commissioned the Goodwood piece, she created her only truly lifelike representation of a horse, but it is still spiritual at heart, a reminder of the long and complex shared history of humans and domesticated animals.

Address Goodwood Racecourse, Chichester, PO18 0PS, +44 (0)1243 755022, www.goodwood.com/horseracing/racecourse | Getting there Train to Chichester station; bus 900 runs twice hourly from Chichester station (North car park) to the racecourse on race days, 10.15am–1.15pm; by car via the A 27 and A 285 | Hours Check website for details of events and opening times | Tip Frink also created sculptures of horses with a rider; see one such sculpture in Worthing, where her Desert Quartet of monumental bronze heads can be found in Liverpool Gardens, near the seafront; further afield, other Frink sculptures can be found on Winchester High Street, and in Bond Street in Mayfair, London.

44 Fishbourne Reed Beds
Stirring vistas channelling nature and novels

The point where the northern tip of Chichester Harbour pushes into the Sussex shore is a magical zone of transition. Rather than a clear break where sea ends and land begins, the Fishbourne Channel dissolves into a skein of briny waterways, where salt marsh merges into a wonderland of soaring reeds.

Reeds are one of the few plants that can survive daily exposure to salt water – in fact they thrive here, rising metres above the tidal flow, whispering with any breeze. A network of walkways and little wooden bridges provides a perfect way to delve into this landscape in search of distinctive wildlife – or just reflect on the magic of nature.

Reed buntings are among year-round avian residents, while bird lovers may also spy pipits and snipes, chiffchaffs and other warblers, as well as waterfowl such as red-breasted mergansers. Give yourself a gold star if you can see through its brown-and-black camouflage plumage to spot a bittern lurking shyly amid the reeds. The reed beds are also home to water voles – listen for the little 'plop' as they dive, or look for cleanly cut reeds which the animals harvest as building material. Look down, too, from the wooden bridges for both salt and freshwater fish sharing the tranquil waters below.

The reed beds also provide a literary pilgrimage for fans of bestselling writer Kate Mosse, who lives nearby, with Fishbourne the backdrop for her novel *The Taxidermist's Daughter*. Though set in the 1910s, the landscape of the story still echoes here, from the characterful thatched houses by the large pond on Mill Lane to the home of two of the novel's protagonists by a lone oak tree that remains where the reeds peter into marsh. Ancient history lurks here too, in the shape of jetties now submerged beneath the pond, dating back two millennia to when the sea reached further inland, and Fishbourne was a key port of Roman Britain.

Address Paths run into the reed beds from behind the pond on Mill Lane, Fishbourne, PO19 3JN | Getting there 15-minute walk from Fishbourne railway station; by car, Mill Lane runs off the A 259; bus 56 runs along the A 259 to Fishbourne | Hours Accessible 24 hours | Tip Enjoy mussels and other seafood at The Bull's Head, a 17th-century pub at the top of Mill Lane that also features in *The Taxidermist's Daughter*.

45 Fishbourne Roman Palace

Ancient high life – with Cupid on a dolphin

It's just a few minutes by train from Chichester to Fishbourne, but that short journey leads to a 2000-year portal back in time. When Chichester was the Roman city of Noviomagus Reginorum, a palatial villa was built as a luxury haven by the waters of Chichester Harbour, when the Fishbourne Channel reached further inland than its dazzling reed beds do today.

Dating to around A.D. 75, this is the largest Roman residence discovered in Britain – as well as Britain's most extensive *in-situ* Roman mosaics. Without title deeds, we can't be certain of its original owner, but one candidate is Tiberius Claudius Cogidubnus, a 1st-century tribal ruler who kept power by playing nice with the new Roman overlords.

Despite its past grandeur – featuring four residential wings around a courtyard garden – the site was discovered only by chance. Mosaic flooring was first uncovered by house builders in 1805 – but, remarkably, ignored as they just carried on building. It wasn't until 1960 that digging for a new water main again uncovered the palace foundations, prompting archaeologists to come and unearth a hidden jewel.

As with any home, changing tastes prompted redecoration. This included overlaying many of the original simple black and white geometric mosaics with more ornate colour designs. The most famous is the perfectly preserved north wing floor featuring Cupid riding on a sea creature, now understood to be a not-quite-accurate depiction of a dolphin. The palace was finally abandoned around A.D. 270, following a devastating fire.

Don't skip the gardens, recreated in past style with hedging planted in the same holes dug by their green-fingered Imperial tenders, alongside apples planted in the Roman-created espalier style. In the far corner, a museum hut provides a further window on ancient gardening practice, framed by a vine-draped courtyard.

Address Roman Way, Chichester, PO19 3QR, www.sussexpast.co.uk | Getting there 10-minute walk from Fishbourne railway station; two miles from central Chichester via the A27; bus 56 towards Old Bosham | Hours Daily mid-Feb–Nov 10am–5pm | Tip The second-hand books room between the main museum and its café may look tiny, but it's jammed with a diverse range of intriguing cultural and history books worth exploring.

14

46 Forbes Place Wisteria
Britain's only Listed shrub

Fans of British architecture and history are familiar with 'Listed' status given to structures of particular architectural and/or historic interest deserving of special protection. But the vast wisteria adorning the façade of Forbes Place – now luxury flats – enjoys unique status as the only Listed bush – as opposed to tree – in the UK. It now stretches nearly 250 yards along the south façade.

The plant was a gift from China's Ambassador to Britain, presented in the mid-1820s, to provide decorative greenery for the opening of what was then the new West Sussex, East Hampshire and Chichester General Infirmary and Dispensary. The building at Forbes Places – itself Grade II listed – marked an expansion of a Public 'Dispensary for Sick Poor' opened by Dr Thomas Sanden in 1784 in three cottages just off Broyle Road.

Though wisteria-clad façades are now an iconic sight across Britain, at the time, this gift from China was a new and sensational horticultural star. The genus Wisteria – gathering different varieties of the plant found worldwide (the Chichester one is *Wisteria sinensis*) – was established by Thomas Nuttall in 1818, but mystery surrounds his naming of the genus. While some say it was in honour of American anatomist Caspar Wistar – whom Nuttall knew during a spell in Philadelphia – others highlight the spelling to suggest it was named after Nuttall's friend, Charles Wister (who was also Wistar's cousin).

Wisteria has been around a long time, with seven million year-old fossils of *Wisteria sinensis* found in China, where it became known as 'Zi Ten' ('Blue vine'). An even older example than the Chichester plant adorns Fuller's Griffin Brewery in London, said to have been planted in 1816 – one of the first pair of saplings brought from China by John Reeves, Chief Inspector of Tea at Canton. The other was planted at London's Kew Gardens, but sadly died.

Address Forbes Place, King George Gardens, Chichester, PO19 6LF | **Getting there** 30-minute walk from Chichester railway station | **Hours** Accessible 24 hours | **Tip** Discover another slice of greenery with a secret history just a mile to the west at Brandy Hole Copse, a beautiful Local Nature Reserve woodland which in addition to its verdant plant life also contains Roman-era defensive ditches, plus rare examples of World War II 'Dragon's Teeth' – obstacles put in place to block German tanks ahead of a feared invasion. The Copse, meanwhile, takes its name from a hoard of smuggled brandy discovered here in the past.

47__Fountain Inn
Chichester's oldest surviving pub

While other older Chichester pubs have called time, the Fountain continues to provide nice drink, affordable food and good cheer, as it has since 1798. The pub embodies an even older past, though. Step inside the formal dining area at the back and you'll find a section of the town's 2000-year-old Roman wall still in fine shape in one corner. The ghost of a Roman soldier is also believed to wander here, among several reputed spectres.

Built where the ancient imperial town's South Gate once stood – it was demolished in 1773 – the Fountain has enjoyed its fair share of stories and characters. There's little detail, alas, of the soldier who found local renown for eating a 'gargantuan meal' here in 1807 to win a bet. But we do know the pub was well known as a hotspot for traditional games such as Singlesticks or Back-sword – which featured a local champion with the memorable name of 'Muff of Lavant'.

More is known about the Fountain's notable landlords. George Neal held the role in the 1830s, and when his daughter Sarah married Kent county cricketer Joseph Wells, they bore a son named Herbert George. He became more familiarly known as H. G. Wells, who combined writing groundbreaking futuristic novels such as *War of the Worlds*, *The Invisible Man* and *The Time Machine* with important works of social commentary.

An air of criminal mystery surrounds another former landlord, Sampson Willcocks. Though he was declared bankrupt by a court on 12 November 1873, that declaration took place with Willcocks absent, as two weeks earlier he and his family had boarded the famous 19th-century cruise ship SS *Great Britain* bound for Australia, using the false name of 'Wilcox'. In 1875, Sampson re-emerged as the new landlord of the Australia Hotel pub in the small New South Wales town of Wallsend – no doubt toasting his escape from British justice.

Specials

Ciabatta: Sausage + Bacon
Soup: Spicy Vegetable
Grazer: Hampshire Steak
Main: Halloumi + Bacon Salad
Dessert: Apple Cake
Cocktail: Gingerbread Espresso Martini

. Ask the team for our
full food & cocktail menu!

FIRES ARE LIKE MEN, THEY GO OUT IF NOT WATCHED.

Upcoming Events

* Follow Us: ?
INSTA: thefountainchi
FB: TheFountainChichester

Address 29 Southgate, Chichester, PO19 1ES, www.fountainchichester.co.uk | **Getting there** 10-minute walk from Chichester railway station | **Hours** Mon–Wed noon–10pm, Thu noon–11pm, Fri & Sat noon–midnight, Sun noon–6pm | **Tip** Though the Fountain Inn is Chichester's oldest remaining pub, the 1750s building that was once home to the Crown pub is still serving customers as a Mexican restaurant called Muchos Nachos (www.muchos-nachos.com)!

48 Fox Hall

Luxurious reminder of bygone country living

Once upon a time, fox hunting was merely a genteel rural sport rather than a matter of heated debate. And for a large part of the 17th and 18th centuries, the village of Charlton was the headquarters of a hunt considered the most fashionable in England. So prestigious was it that even the grand Goodwood Estate was often described simply as being 'near Charlton'.

The Charlton Hunt was founded in the 1670s by the Duke of Monmouth, and continued after his death by his son-in-law, the Duke of Bolton, and then by the Duke of Richmond. Contemporary records show that, while many gentlemen who rode with the hunt had to be content with accommodation in local inns, the grandest sought something more private and luxurious – a place such as Fox Hall, built in 1730 for the 2nd Duke of Richmond, joint-Master of the Charlton Hunt.

Given his elite status, it's no surprise the Duke commissioned a place worthy of bragging rights, and this stunning Palladian-style hunting lodge ticks all the boxes. Even better, Fox Hall is available for anyone to stay in today, part of the portfolio of characterful historic lodgings overseen by the Landmark Trust.

The elegant simplicity of its brick exterior belies the exuberance within. Entering past utilitarian servants' rooms on the ground floor, a staircase leads to the opulent apartment set aside for the Duke, which has been described as Britain's grandest bedsitter. Thoughtfully, the room was ready to welcome the Duchess if she chose to visit, featuring a powder-closet off to one side. But a detail over the fireplace provides a reminder of the main purpose of being here – a wind indicator to tell the Master of the Hunt how the scent of his prey would be lying, to aid planning the day's chase. A new weather vane installed in 2010 ensures the indicator works perfectly again today – though now the local foxes can rest easy.

Address Charlton, West Sussex, PO18 1 HZ | Getting there By car via the A 286 |
Hours Exterior accessible 24 hours; also available to rent via the Landmark Trust:
www.landmarktrust.org.uk | Tip The Fox Goes Free is a fine nearby 400-year-old country
pub – with grand country views from its beer garden (www.thefoxgoesfree.com).

49 Guildhall

Where a poet faced death

Rising from the green expanse of Priory Park in the heart of Chichester, the beautiful ancient stone building now known as the Guildhall was once the chapel of the Franciscan Order, commonly known as the 'Grey Friars'. The holy men received the land that now forms the park from Richard, Earl of Cornwall, in 1269, with the first record of today's edifice being the ordination of an archbishop in 1283. It is one of the few Franciscan friaries in England to have retained its roof following the destruction that went with the dissolution of the monasteries under Henry VIII.

Perhaps the Guildhall's most notable appearance in the limelight, however, came in 1804, when illustrious poet and visionary William Blake was tried here for sedition. Blake's 'crime' may seem minor by today's standards – more a fit of temper than something that at the time carried a death sentence. He was accused of evicting drunken soldiers from his cottage garden at Felpham with the words 'Damn the King, damn the country and damn you too!'. Thankfully for future generations, Blake was afforded representation by the best legal team available, and acquitted.

Cricket matches between local teams provide a wonderful summer bonus for visitors to the Guildhall's surrounding park, though for many decades Priory Park was a venue for first class matches, starting in 1852, when Sussex took on an All-England XI. In 1882 and 1886 the touring Australian team played on the ground, taking on first Lord March's XI, then a team named United Eleven, which included the legendary W. G. Grace.

Sussex continued playing County Championship Cricket beside the Guildhall until 1950. In 2017, radar revealed two Roman town houses buried near the Guildhall, including remains of a hot room and baths – built centuries before one of England's most famous poets found himself in hot legal waters.

Address Priory Park, Priory Road, Chichester, PO19 1NS | **Getting there** 20-minute walk from Chichester railway station | **Hours** Tue–Fri 10am–4.30pm, Sat 10am–5pm | **Tip** If you'd like to watch – or take part in – a cricket match in the park, you can find out more through the Priory Park Cricket Club (www.priorypark.play-cricket.com).

50__Guitars To Go
No fret in rock guitar heaven

Rock guitarists may have a reputation for flamboyance, but it would be all too easy to miss this distinctive shop, run by musician Trevor Nobes, tucked down a lane between the bustle of North Street and the leafy attractions of Priory Park. The roots of Guitars To Go stretch back a decade, when Trevor was just a keen collector who had amassed 'hundreds' of instruments dating back to the 1960s – until he ran out of money!

At the time, the space had a very different existence as a coffee and cake shop run by one of Trevor's friends and his wife – but when the couple split up, the friend called Trevor and suggested that, as he had 'no money and loads of guitars', he should give the shop space a new use.

As cake shop stuff was moved out, Trevor moved his guitar collection in to provide initial stock – though like most collectors, he admits there were some instruments he didn't want to sell. Thankfully, word soon spread, and the ensuing years have seen a steady stream of customers bringing in guitars to sell or part-exchange, as well as chatting about a shared passion. 'Almost everyone's got more guitars than they know what to do with,' Trevor reveals wryly.

There are always rarities in the shop's eye-catchingly diverse stock, ranging from a rare Les Paul that was produced in a limited edition run of a hundred or so, to quirky creations such as a white plastic Maccafferi guitar made in the early 1950s – to which Trevor has attached a label stating 'This is not a toy'!

Guitars To Go isn't only a meeting place for guitar enthusiasts, but a draw for youngsters dazzled by the old-school cool of the instruments. Some of the younger visitors tell Trevor his shop is like a wonderful musical museum. Yet, in the same way that sports cars deserve to be driven, guitars aren't just objects to look at, so Trevor regularly combines shop work with guest slots for local bands.

Address 3 Guildhall Street, Chichester, PO19 1NJ | **Getting there** 20-minute walk from Chichester railway station | **Hours** Mon–Sat 10.30am–5.30pm | **Tip** Check out the listings for the nearby Chichester Inn, an 18th-century pub hosting regular live music nights (www.chichesterinn.co.uk).

51 Halnaker Mill and Lane
A Middle Earth summit trail

Today, Halnaker (pronounced Ha'naker) is an off-radar clutch of farming businesses north-east of Chichester, surrounded by the South Downs National Park. But it provides the gateway to a ravishing walk along an ancient Roman road to a poetic windmill.

Where Warehead Farm stands today, head north-east up the right hand fork of two lanes by the farm, and you'll find yourself on the route of ancient Stane Street, which two millennia ago was the Roman road from Chichester to London. Its most iconic stretch soon appears, in the shape of a spectacular tunnel of trees arching over the path. As you traverse this magical section, it's easy to imagine yourself as a Tolkien character striding through The Shire in Middle Earth.

Carry on through the tunnel of trees and follow the footpath turning north as it climbs to the summit of a hill, on top of which stands the gorgeous Halnaker Mill, commanding a viewpoint with spectacular vistas, on a clear day as far as the distant sea to the south. At your feet, meanwhile, look out for rare Downland orchids dotting the chalky earth.

The first windmill here was built for the Duke of Richmond and the Goodwood Estate around 1540, but the present Grade II-listed beauty dates to the mid 1700s. It was a working mill, grinding flour for the local area until being abandoned after being struck by lightning in 1905. The abandoned mill inspired a lovely but melancholy 1923 poem by famed Sussex poet Hillaire Belloc, which proclaimed: 'Ha'nacker Hill is in Desolation: Ruin a-top and a field unploughed,' and concluded with a reflection on wider loss in the line: 'Ha'nacker's down and England's done.'

The whole area at the top of Halnaker Hill is, however, a Scheduled Ancient Monument, as it also hosts a Neolithic earthwork enclosure. There's also a World War II radio wave direction-finding structure used to track German aircraft.

Address Windmill Trail, Chichester, PO18 0QS | Getting there By car, via the A285 four miles north-east of Chichester, with limited parking by Warehead farm, accessed by taking Stane Street (be sure to avoid blocking access to the farm); bus 55 towards Tangmere runs from Chichester Cathedral to the nearby Halnaker Crossroads, via the Anglesey Arms pub, from where the Mill is a 20-minute walk | Hours Accessible 24 hours | Tip Taste award-winning local wines at the nearby Tinwood Estate vineyard, signposted just off the A285, home to a restaurant and three luxury lodges (www.tinwoodestate.com).

52_John Marsh House
Remembering a forgotten English musical maestro

Perhaps now known only to fervent musicologists, John Marsh was almost certainly the most prolific English composer of the Georgian era – credited with over 350 compositions, including at least 39 symphonies. A lawyer by training, Marsh was largely self-taught as a musician, becoming proficient at several instruments, including violin and viola.

Marsh was born in 1752 in the Surrey town of Dorking, and lived in several places around south-east England before settling in Chichester in 1787, where he lived until his death in 1828. Of Marsh's symphonies, only nine he published himself are now extant, and experts have compared them to the work of Handel and J. C. Bach. They also constitute some of the only surviving English symphonies from the period. Other works by Marsh include three one-movement finales, several sets of organ voluntaries for teaching student organists, and a dozen unpublished pieces he described as 'Full Concertoes in the ancient style'.

While Marsh's music lay in obscurity for nearly two centuries, he has recently enjoyed a limited revival of interest. A key spur to this are 37 volumes of journals he wrote about society in his time, which were published in 1998 under the title *The John Marsh Journals—The Life and Times of a Gentleman Composer*. They are now considered one of the most valuable sources of insight into life and music in 18th-century England. Marsh's other writings include an essay entitled *Hints to Young Composers*.

One notable recording from 1989 featured works by Marsh clustered under the label The Chichester Symphonies, played on copies of 18th-century instruments. Works included Symphony No. 4 in F Major (1788), Symphony No. 7 in E-flat Major (*La Chasse*) (1790) and Symphony No. 6 in D Major (1796). Marsh's house seems to have been a hotspot for Georgian creativity – it had previously been home to the poet William Hayley.

Address 7 North Pallant, Chichester, PO19 1TQ | Getting there 15-minute walk from Chichester railway station | Hours Viewable from outside only | Tip Musicians inspired by Marsh's story can find sheet music galore in the nearby Ackerman's Music shop, 42 West Street.

53 John Piper Tapestry

A glorious covering for a drab bit of wood

Looking around Chichester Cathedral in the early 1960s, contemporary art-loving Dean, Walter Hussey, decided the area around the high altar looked rather drab and gloomy. A dark 16th-century oak reredos – an ornamental screen placed behind an altar – didn't help. Seeking an artist to provide something colourful for the spot, Hussey sought advice from Henry Moore – and the illustrious sculptor suggested John Piper.

Piper described the commission as 'in some ways the most frightening' he had ever received – as tapestry was a medium he had never previously attempted. Despite this, Piper decided to create an ambitious work occupying the whole area behind the altar – though he teamed up with expert French weavers Pinton Freres to help ensure a good result.

The theme chosen for the tapestry consisted of symbols of the Trinity in the central portion, with depictions of the four Classical elements (earth, air, fire and water) and the beasts associated with the Evangelists (the man for Matthew, lion for Mark, ox for Luke and eagle for John) on either side. By the end of 1964, Piper had a draft of the work ready to go – though last-minute changes had to be made after Lancelot Mason, Archdeacon of Chichester, objected to Piper's choice of certain symbols, which he deemed confusing.

The resulting masterpiece – unveiled at Evensong on 20 September 1966 – features seven panels, each one a metre wide and five metres high, draped across the drab old reredos. Though Hussey was delighted with its dazzling colour, others were much less keen. Complaints poured in to the local press, echoed by members of the congregation who said the tapestry was so garish they would not take Communion before it. The most famous objector was Cheslyn Jones – Canon Chancellor at the Cathedral – who reportedly wore dark glasses to the dedication service! You can't please everyone.

Address Chichester Cathedral, Chichester, PO19 1PX, www.chichestercathedral.org.uk | **Getting there** 10-minute walk from Chichester railway station | **Hours** Mon–Sat 9am–5pm, Sun 12.30–2.30pm | **Tip** Look closely at the 'air' motif in the tapestry, and decide whether you agree with suggestions that Piper may have been influenced by the shape of Sputnik I (the first artificial satellite, launched in 1957) in creating that element.

54 J Voke Vintage Tearoom
Old style cuppas – plus a headlining host

Tucked away off the end of East Street is a distinctive spot for an intriguing cuppa which, until it hit national headlines in 2020, seemed almost secretive. There's little to even tell you what the place is, until you notice an engraved window promising a 'Vintage Tea Room and Emporium for Fine Gentlemen and Ladies of Today'. Peer in, though, and there's no sign of a tearoom – just a ramshackle front space selling a hotch-potch of retro items.

The tearoom is down steps at the back, where a cosy wood-panelled parlour – warmed in winter by a Victorian fireplace – is the backdrop for sipping Michael Schneider's menu of distinctive leaf teas, such as smokily fragrant Russian Caravan, Japanese Sencha or Taiwanese Longjin. All come artfully served in vintage china. One typical review summed up its appeal: 'Excellent afternoon tea in strange surroundings. Host very attentive. Funny and entertaining.'

'I have vintage items in the window to tempt people in – things people bring in to sell,' says Schneider. The frontage is vintage too, with Schneider claiming it to be the oldest shop sign in Chichester, dating back to 1891. As to the name, it refers to Voke's Tearoom, which operated next door in the early decades of the last century.

'We are a refuge from all the hustle and bustle of the outside world,' Schneider told local press on opening in 2017. But in 2020, J Voke became the centre of a media storm when, during the UK's first COVID lockdown, he put a poster in the window decrying the wearing of face masks, which he called 'Government muzzles'. Police were called, and tabloid papers claimed he was 'banning' mask wearers. Schneider said he only wanted to share his opinion, and that if someone said a mask made them feel safer that was fine with him. Ironically, the headlines sparked a surge in customers! Something to discuss over a cup of tea, perhaps. Joanna's in The Buttermarket provides a shinier retro café contrast.

Address 8 The Hornet, Chichester, PO19 7JG | Getting there 20-minute walk from Chichester railway station | Hours Mon–Sat 8.30am–4.30pm | Tip If you like the Royal Doulton and other antique crockery at J Voke, walk a little further down The Hornet to scour for some of your own at Squirrel Antiques.

55 — Keats' Seat
Poetic vision with unexpected piggy link

Set on Eastgate Square in 2017, Vincent Gray's evocative bronze of John Keats welcomes company on a bench by the house where one of England's most famous poets enjoyed a productive visit – acknowledged by a grey slate plaque on the building diagonally opposite where he stayed. Gray's statue is designed for people to sit by Keats, and follow the poet's gaze down East Street to Chichester's medieval Market Cross and Cathedral spire beyond.

These landmarks both appear in The Eve of St Agnes, the celebrated poem Keats began during his 1819 visit. He arrived on 20 January – the eve of the Catholic holy day for the patron saint of virgins, martyred in 4th-century Rome. The Eve of St Agnes tells a familiar story of two young lovers driven apart by feuding families. The poem's innocent heroine – Madeline – goes to bed on the holy day eve, setting her eyes to Heaven to encourage dreams of her future husband.

The medieval architecture that dominated Chichester when Keats visited seems to have inspired the great hall and house where Madeline resides in the poem. And there are clues pointing to a particular building. Keats wrote to his brother George about invitations to card parties with 'old dowagers', including a Mrs Mary Lacy, who lived in a 12th-century building that was formerly the Guildhall. Her rooms would have been directly above a huge vaulted cellar now known as the crypt, whose grandeur fits Keats' description in the poem of Porphyra, Madeline's courtly lover, standing in a great hall 'hid from the torch's flame, Behind a broad hall-pillar […] He follow'd through a lowly arched way, Brushing the cobwebs with his lofty plume'.

Before Keats' time, the landlord of the White Horse Inn on South Street leased the vaults from 1661 for the ostensible purpose of storing wine – though in 1686 there were complaints pigs were being kept there too!

Address Eastgate Square, Chichester, PO19 1JN | **Getting there** 20-minute walk from Chichester railway station | **Hours** Accessible 24 hours | **Tip** Browse a selection of second-hand poetry books – and much else – in the excellent Oxfam charity bookshop a short stroll away along East Street.

56 Market Cross

Meeting point for people and history

One of only two remaining Market Crosses in Sussex – the other is the much smaller affair in Alfriston – Chichester's central meeting point was built around 1501 by Bishop Edward Story, who paid ten pounds to the Mayor of Chichester for the ground on which it's built. Today's Cross was built on the site of an earlier wooden construction, erected in the 14th century where Chichester's original Roman roads met. The current octagonal Cross is made of Caen stone, with a central column supported by eight flying buttresses. Low stone seats embrace the column, while its arches feature carvings depicting things like a bishop's mitre and demi-angels.

The bishop built the cross to provide a place where poorer peasants with only a small amount of produce to sell could still offer their wares to passers-by without paying a market trader toll – provided they stood in the blessedly free shelter of the cross. Trading continued here for 400 years until the creation of a larger market site in the shape of today's Butter Market 100 metres away up North Street. At this point, some members of the council actually called for the Market Cross to be demolished, though wiser colleagues thankfully stepped in to save it.

The cross has not always escaped harm, though. In 1642, for example, major damage was done to statues adorning the structure during the Civil War, which saw Chichester attacked as a royalist stronghold. Even when its traders had left, the cross remained a focal point for social interactions, and was often the venue for brawling during the 17th and 18th centuries.

The stone orb and accompanying weather vane had to be removed in 2014 when the supporting structure began to crack. Artwork on the vane had also worn away, but a chance encounter led to restorers tracking down its most recent painter, Ian Harris, who was able to redo the work.

Address Market Cross, Chichester, PO19 1HH | Getting there 10-minute walk from Chichester railway station | Hours Accessible 24 hours | Tip A golden crowned bust of King Charles I by Hubert Le Sueur – originally sculptor to King Louis XIII of France before moving to England – was added to the cross in the 1660s, but removed in the 1970s. It can now be seen in all its glory in the nearby Novium Museum (www.thenovium.org).

57 Minerva Mural

Impressive Roman goddess on quiet display

It would be all too easy for people walking up the busy North Street to miss this ravishing tiled mural by Yvonne Hudson Rusbridge, bringing a fascinating slice of ancient mythology to a corner of Sussex House on Crane Street.

Standing around four metres tall and one metre wide, the mural features 36 ceramic coloured tiles with raised surfaces. The main figure is a stylised standing profile of Minerva – the Roman goddess of crafts, poetry and wisdom, also credited as being the inventor of music. There was no end to her reputed talents, however, as Minerva also served as a goddess of warriors, medicine and wisdom, as well as providing go-to inspiration in the arts, trade and strategy.

Our goddess is accompanied here by a host of avian companions. Her gaze tracks the flight of a departing swift, and there's a lapwing on the ground plus an owl perched on her shoulder. Other birds depicted include chough, crow, herring gull, curlew, bittern, kestrel, sparrowhawk, cormorant and swallow. To add to her mystique, mythology decrees that Minerva sprang fully grown from inside the head of the god Jupiter, when fellow deity Vulcan opened up his skull to treat a terrible headache. The story adds that Minerva was born ready for action, dressed in armour beneath a long robe, and bearing a helmet, shield and spear.

Mystery surrounds the date of the mural's creation. Whilst Public Sculptures of Sussex quotes one of the artist's children saying it was possibly created for the opening of the nearby Minerva Theatre in 1989, most art historians believe it was made in the 1970s as a pleasing nod to Chichester's Roman roots. Although a Londoner by birth, the artist lived in Sussex for much of her life after marrying farmer John Rusbridge in 1949, settling in the village of Earnley near Chichester – where she created two striking ceramic panels in its 13th-century church.

Address Corner of Crane Street and North Street, Chichester, PO19 1LJ | Getting there 20-minute walk from Chichester railway station | Hours Accessible 24 hours | Tip Yvonne Rusbridge Hudson also created tapestries, and you can admire one depicting five Sussex saints in Birdham Church near Chichester, plus an altar cloth depicting St Richard feeding the hungry of Chichester in West Wittering Church.

58__Noir Mural

A poppy splash of Berlin and The Beatles

Pity the car drivers unable to fully take in this eye-catching mural as they make their way around the busy North Gate Roundabout. Covering a giant section of Metro House, the towering work by renowned street artist Thierry Noir presents four boldly coloured cartoonish faces that pay homage to characters in The Beatles' 1968 animated film *Yellow Submarine.*

Though the mural brings a delightful dash of retro pop psychedelia to Chichester, Noir is most closely associated with Berlin. Born in the French city of Lyon in 1958, he moved to Germany in 1982, and acquired legendary status for being among the first – if not *the* first – artist to paint the western side of the Berlin Wall. This was both an act of free expression and a form of protest against the restrictive Communist dictatorship on the East German side. 'I did nothing but react to its sadness,' Noir once said.

Painting on the Wall was strictly forbidden at the time – it had been built three metres beyond the official border so that East German guards were able to arrest any person standing too near it. Noir responded by learning to paint fast, using a technique he described as 'two ideas, three colours'. Noir's deceptively simple characters and visual language gained iconic status, and his work was immortalised in both Wim Wenders' acclaimed 1987 film *Wings of Desire* and on the cover of U2's album *Achtung Baby*.

His presence here is down to the Chichester Street Art festival in 2013, which saw work by a host of international artists appear around the town, after being organised in secret for a year beforehand by Street Art London and the National Open Art Competition. 'The art will be up as long as people don't want it taken down, as long as there is no outcry,' said National Open Art Competition CEO Lawson Baker to the Chichester Observer in 2014. And despite some decriers, here it remains.

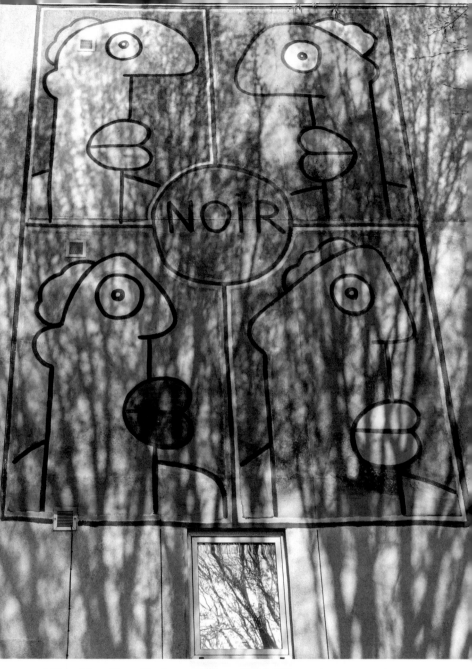

Address Metro House, Northgate, Chichester, PO19 1BE, www.instagram.com/thierrynoir | Getting there 25-minute walk from Chichester railway station | Hours Accessible 24 hours | Tip There's also an incredible – and very different – 2013 mural by Spanish artist Liqen around the corner of Metro House, on its west side.

59 North Bersted Man

Memorable human contact with the Iron Age

Ahead of the building of a housing estate in Bersted (just north of Bognor Regis) in 2008, a group of archaeologists took the opportunity to explore ditches and pits opened up in readiness of construction starting. They were stunned to come across the grave of the most elaborately equipped Iron Age warrior ever found in England, whose body and trappings now form one of the most evocative displays at the Novium Museum.

Years of analysis and conservation preceded 'North Bersted Man' going on public view – with brilliantly recreated accoutrements, and fascinating details of who he had been. Isotopic analysis, for example, pointed to his having lived in the first century before Christ, while clues from both biology and costume pointed to his being French Gallic – most likely a warrior fleeing Julius Caesar's Roman legions as they swept across continental Europe around 50 B.C.

Aged around 45 at time of death, analysis suggested he stood around 1.7 metres (5 feet 7 inches) tall. He was also clearly a man of importance, laid to rest with burial rites showing honour and respect. For example, both the sword and striking bronze shield found with the body had been carefully broken in a ceremonial manner that represented the ritual 'killing' of his weaponry. His spear had also been broken, and the spearhead placed by his head.

The most striking element of the burial is the helmet that sat on that head – one of only four Iron Age helmets discovered in Britain. While it certainly provided protection in battle, the breathtaking and intricately crafted plumed crest the helmet bore – made from animal hair or feathers – is proof that its wearer was an individual of huge status. Incredibly rare in Britain, such crested items are more associated with Iron Age French sites – further evidence that this mystery warrior was a traveller who found final peace in the Sussex earth.

Address Novium Museum, 1 Tower Street, Chichester, PO19 1QH, www.thenovium.org | Getting there 20-minute walk from Chichester railway station | Hours Tue–Fri 10am–4.30pm, Sat 10am–5pm, Sun 10am–4pm | Tip You can seen an online film made by The Novium about the discovery and long conservation work that brought the North Bersted Man display to life: www.thenovium.org/mysterywarrior.

60 Oxmarket Gallery

Contemporary art worshipped in an ancient church

Tucked away down a slender lane off the bustle of East Street is a deconsecrated medieval church that today celebrates an ever-changing roster of intriguing contemporary artists from around the region, working in a range of media. The building that was formerly St Andrew-in-the-Oxmarket has existed since the 13th century, and was used as a church continuously until being badly damaged by German bombs in 1943, forcing its congregation to decamp to the nearby All Saints-in-the-Pallant. The church was then deconsecrated in the 1950s.

After a couple of decades of melancholy abandonment, the art-loving 1960s Archdeacon of Chichester, Lancelot Mason – working alongside Walter Hussey, the art commissioning Dean of Chichester Cathedral – proposed turning the church into a gallery, as the town lacked a dedicated exhibition space in those pre-Pallant House days. Restored in the early 1970s, the space opened as the Chichester Centre of Arts in 1976, and then the Oxmarket Centre of Arts before taking on its present name.

Boasting a Grade II listing from Historic England, the Oxmarket has altered shape at various points over the centuries. Additions to the church were made in the 14th, 15th and 19th centuries, and it was extended further in 1989 using rubble stone. In 2020, a major makeover saw the interior modernised and a new enlarged entrance created.

Period mementoes abound. The north window of the church depicts St Cecilia, and the south window of the church has a tribute to poet William Collins, who is buried within the church. The stonework includes reused fragments of herringbone pattern work from Norman times, as well as rubble taken from the demolished Roman walls around the city centre. The windows date back as far as the 13th century. On the 19th-century timber roof, meanwhile, is a weatherboarded bell-cot topped with a short broach spire.

Address St Andrews Court, Chichester, PO19 1YH, www.oxmarket.org | Getting there 15-minute walk from Chichester railway station; buses to the Market Cross | Hours Tue–Sun 10am–4.30pm | Tip Find more commercial international art on show at the Whitewall Gallery, just a stone's throw away on East Street.

61 Roundhill Picture Palace

Unique cinema that proves bigger isn't always better

The story of how one of the world's smallest cinemas came to Chichester would make a nice subject for a film in itself. With up to 13 seats available – staggered in height and with ample leg room – the whole thing sits within a tailor-made shepherd's hut built by a family duo with a keen eye for evocative, historic style.

Sister and brother Louise and Paul Adams have been building unique examples of these traditional wagons at their workshop in East Dean since 2009. Whilst exhibiting their shepherd's huts at a show, they came across a 1950s thresher machine axle base with wheels that a farmer wanted to sell – though after snapping it up, it sat gathering dust and rust while the duo wondered how best to use it.

Then Louise saw a TV programme about a vintage 1960s mobile cinema, itself a nod to touring cinematograph shows that toured the country with travelling fairs in the early 20th century. She was also inspired by two dramas – one of which showcased vintage 19th-century shop fronts, plus the period film *Anna Karenina*. Louise says she had 'a light bulb moment'. Why not build a travelling picture palace with an opulent but cosy interior redolent of elegant past times, featuring plush carpets, fluted columns, cherub uplighters, plus hand-painted murals featuring classic scenes from diverse film, ranging from Westerns and thrillers to epic adventures? Louise sourced seats from an old cinema in Dorset, alongside other items such as Art Deco lights and reclaimed cupboards. Other quirky items included a 19th-century Italian head, whose face provided moulds to create a set of masks that were then given a sheen of golden gilding. The screening equipment, though, is state-of-the-art – and alongside film programmes ranging from vintage silents to modern spectaculars, the venue hosts other events ranging from book readings to instrumental recitals.

Address New Park Road, Chichester, PO19 7XY, www.newparkcentre.org.uk | Getting there 25-minute walk from Chichester railway station | Hours Available for private hire, as well as public screenings at events such as the annual Chichester Film Festival, held over three weeks in August | Tip See other examples of Roundhill Shepherd Huts at the family workshop in East Dean, north of Chichester, open daily 10am–5pm daily (www.roundhillshepherdhuts.co.uk).

62 — Shippam's Wishbone Sign

A savoury story with wishes attached

Shippam's has been a flavoursome presence in Chichester since 1750, when Sergeant Shipston Shippam opened a grocery shop at West Gate. The eye-catching, wishbone-adorned sign nods to the factory and second shop that opened on East Street in 1783. The business flourished after securing a deal to help feed the Royal Navy dockyard and ships along the coast at Portsmouth during the Napoleonic Wars (1803–1815).

A move into pastes and sandwich spreads – along with canned and jarred meats, plus soups – was underpinned by an array of fine, globally sourced ingredients. As one 19th-century ad set out: 'There are sardines from Portugal, anchovies from Spain, salmon from Canada and the United States, lobster from Nova Scotia, shrimps from Holland, prawns from Scandinavia and turtles from Bermuda.' As well as turtle soup, another of Shippam's distinctive Victorian gourmet offerings was 'Galantine of Wild Boar's Head with Pistachio Kernels'.

In 1948, Shippam's was honoured with a Royal Warrant as Suppliers of Meat and Fish Pastes first to George VI, then Elizabeth II. The company was a leader in the field of advertising too, becoming one of the first to launch a television advert in 1955. One upmarket cinema ad that year, entitled *Shippam's Guide to Opera*, won an award at the Monte Carlo Film Advertising Festival. The Novium Museum on Tower Street has a fascinating collection of memorabilia and photographs chronicling the history of Shippam's.

Production continued at East Street until 2002, when it moved to a factory on Terminus Road. The giant wishbone hanging beneath the East Street sign alludes to the vast number that are produced as a by-product of the business, amounting to an average of around 1,200 new wishbones generated each day. In an admirable example of 'waste not, want not', locals were encouraged to drop by and pick wishbones up as good luck tokens.

Address 48 East Street, Chichester, PO19 1HX | Getting there 15-minute walk from Chichester railway station; buses to the Market Cross | Hours Visible 24 hours | Tip Vietnamese bánh mì, spring rolls and Asian-inspired chicken dishes at Saigon Munchbox offer a distinctive Chichester snack option in an unexpected spot – southside platform 2 at Chichester railway station!

63 — South Downs Planetarium

Cosy setting for inspiring cosmic exploration

Carved from an old barn on former farmland just south of Chichester station, the planetarium was the brainchild of the South Downs Astronomical Society to bring cosmic wonders to this corner of Sussex. Though first conceived in 1992, it was a decade before the planetarium was finally opened by legendary British TV astronomer Sir Patrick Moore, and the then Astronomer Royal, Sir Martin Rees.

In the building that now bears Sir Patrick's name, you can gaze at a panoply of around 4,500 stars and other celestial objects projected onto the dome of a 96-seat auditorium, with commentaries provided by professional astronomers. The building also has a science centre providing context for the dazzling visuals, plus a collection of crash-landed space rocks donated by the British and Irish Meteorite Society. For the technically minded, the indoor celestial panoply is created by a Viewlex-Minolta S-IIb star projector dating back to the 1970s, and acquired from the Armagh Planetarium in Ireland, having been put aside for several years after breaking down. Diligent work by astronomer Dr John Mason thankfully returned it to fine fettle.

As well as events for schools, it's pleasing to discover that even in the era of GPS, the planetarium provides valuable practical training to the Royal Navy and other maritime services in the field of astro navigation. There are also teacher training courses for university students aiming to teach sciences, and lessons for people keen to learn how to use a telescope. And when the weather allows, the planetarium team offers outdoor sessions to view the heavens directly.

Themes for regular monthly shows include 'A Tour of the Planets', 'Magnificent Moons', 'Springtime Stars and Galaxies' and 'The Hunt for Earth-like Planets'. There are also events featuring images beamed a million miles back to Earth from the James Webb Space Telescope.

Address High School Campus, Sir Patrick Moore Building, off Kingsham Road, Chichester, PO19 8RP, www.southdowns.org.uk | Getting there Train to Chichester railway station, then a 10-minute walk | Hours Planetarium opens 45 minutes before each event | Tip If you're inspired to get a telescope yourself, Sussex Astronomy Centre in Goring-by-Sea, 18 miles east of Chichester, sells a wide selection (www.sussex-astronomy-centre.co.uk).

64 Spartacus
Art inspired by a remarkable career change

Rising from the grass outside the entrance to Chichester Festival Theatre, this 2.4 metre-high bronze by Tom Merrifield takes its cues from a dance in the 1950s ballet *Spartacus*, created by Armenian composer Aram Khachaturian. The piece was inspired by a London performance of the work by the Bolshoi Ballet. Erected in 1988, it is just one example of the work of an artist who enjoyed a unique relationship with his subject, as for many years, Merrifield himself was a professional dancer.

Born in Sydney, Merrifield trained in ballet from a young age, becoming a soloist with the Australia-based Borovansky Ballet at 16. In 1956, he moved to Britain, and secured work as a principal dancer with the English National Ballet in London. He also grabbed roles on stage in musicals such as *On the Town* and *West Side Story*, as well as appearing on TV and in films. It was while shooting the classic 1968 movie *Chitty Chitty Bang Bang*, that Merrifield began drawing his fellow dancers. After a cartilage operation made dancing painful, he turned to sculpture – producing the model for his first figure in bronze whilst also being principal dancer in the West End musical *Showboat*.

Merrifield became a full-time artist, however, in the early 1970s, creating sculptures of many of the world's most famous dancers, including Alicia Markova, Anton Dolin and Wayne Sleep, among his subjects. His work has been recognised by the Royal Society of British Sculptors, as well as being exhibited and sold around the world. There are life-sized pieces by Merrifield outside London's Festival Hall and the Victorian Arts Centre in Melbourne, as well as venues in the USA.

Despite the acclaim he drew as a sculptor in the decades before his death in 2021, Merrifield never lost passion for his first career, saying that he 'never gave up dancing but continued to dance through another medium'.

Address Beside Chichester Festival Theatre, Oaklands Way, Chichester, PO19 6AP |
Getting there Train to Chichester railway station then a 25-minute walk | Hours Accessible
24 hours | Tip Take time to admire the statue outside the adjacent Minerva Theatre,
depicting Roman goddess patron of the arts, Minerva. It was made by sculptor Philip Henry
Christopher Jackson to honour Leslie Evershed Martin, a key driving force in founding the
Festival Theatre in 1962 under the artistic directorship of Laurence Olivier.

65 St Mary's Hospital

A unique medieval hospital still providing care

While its soaring barn-like roof and ancient chimneys rise above a girdling of walls at the heart of Chichester, there's nothing to indicate the remarkable nature of St Mary's. For this is one of the world's very few original examples of a medieval hospital – though it had to survive a near miss when a German bomb left a large crater in its garden in 1944.

Dating back to the 13th century, St Mary's is only beaten for the title of oldest hospital in Britain by two in London: St Barts (founded 1123) and the pioneering mental hospital founded as the Priory of St Mary of Bethlehem in 1247, but soon commonly known by the more chilling nickname of 'Bedlam'. A little sign above a black wooden door on St Martin's Square proclaims: 'The Hospital of the Blessed Virgin Mary Founded A.D. 1158–1170', but this refers to a building located between East Street and South Street. However, this was deemed too bustling, prompting a site swap with the Franciscan Friars, who moved from the square to the Guildhall in Priory Park.

Medieval care – carried out by holy brothers and sisters – enforced strict codes for what was effectively a monastic establishment, with hospital inmates deemed guilty of bad behaviour liable to punishments including flogging or expulsion! In 1528, the wonderfully named Dean William Fleshmonger changed St Mary's from hospital to almshouse, caring for those 'worn down with age and infirmity'. In the 17th century, the building housed eight women in their own apartments, but from 1905 both men and married couples could stay.

St Mary's remains virtually as it was originally constructed, with a vast 25-metre-wide timber-framed Great Hall stretching nearly 60 metres to a chapel at the end, separated from the hall by a carved oak screen. There are still four permanent residents – enjoying perhaps the most unique historic care setting in Britain.

Address St Martin's Square, Chichester, PO19 1NR, www.stmarysalmshouses.org.uk, supportteam@stmarysalmshouses.org.uk | Getting there 25-minute walk from Chichester railway station | Hours Accessible by tour Apr–Nov, third Thu of month 1–3pm | Tip Get a further taste of holy inspiration in an ancient setting at the nearby St Olav's, an 11th-century church now turned into an atmospheric religious bookshop (www.stolavchristianbookshop.uk).

66__ St Richard Statue
Devout reformer continues to stand proud

This statue of St Richard, patron saint of Sussex, commemorates a key figure in Chichester's history, whose clean-up of the Church earned both plaudits and fierce opposition. Created by sculptor Philip Jackson in Portland stone – also used in buildings as varied as Buckingham Palace and the United Nations HQ in New York – it was unveiled in 2000.

Clasping a scourge – a symbol of self-discipline – in his left hand, Richard's stony manifestation captures the reformist activism of a 13th-century figure who bravely resisted pressure from both the monarch and his own clergy to root out and stop church corruption. This included prohibiting the then common practice of clergy keeping mistresses, as well as banning the use of Bibles for divination rituals, known as 'sortilegy'.

Richard battled powerful opponents to his reforms. For example, following his consecration by the Pope as Bishop of Chichester in 1245, England's king Henry III barred Richard from both the cathedral and the city! For two years, Richard lived in exile outside the town, until the king overturned the ban. During his life, Richard was linked to various miracles, which helped earn him sainthood within just a few years of his death in 1253. Many of these events concerned apparent defiance of the laws of physics. One referred to an incident at Cakeham Manor on the nearby Selsey peninsular when winds blew out all the candles during an outdoor procession – before Richard's candle mysteriously relit. Another claims that Richard dropped the chalice containing consecrated wine during a service, yet none of the wine was spilled.

Even after death, St Richard inspired antagonism. His former tomb in the cathedral – a shrine that drew many pilgrims each year – was demolished and removed on the orders of Thomas Cromwell as part of his reformation of religion in 1538. There is no record of where Richard's remains were taken.

Address West Street, Chichester, PO19 1PX | Getting there 15-minute walk from Chichester railway station | Hours Accessible 24 hours | Tip There's another statue of St Richard – created by Harry Hems in 1894 – set in the porch on the south side of the cathedral.

67 — Surrealist Trees
Homages to a unique art patron

West Dean is home to one of Britain's most distinctive gardens – notable not just for the diversity of its vast estate, but also artistic imprints in its landscape. That's down to the mark left by Edward James, a pioneering patron of the Surrealist art movement.

His passion for surrealism took local shape when, faced with a pair of dying trees in the Spring Gardens, rather than leave them to rot or be felled, James decided to have the standing timber encased in fibreglass to create a permanent artistic memorial. He commissioned Ralph Burton to create these strange arboreal sculptures in the early 1970s. With the timber eventually rotting away, only the fibreglass shells remain.

The Surrealist Trees contrast with the Regency style of the rest of the Spring Gardens, including lovely little flint bridges and an early 19th-century thatched summerhouse decorated with moss, seaweed and heather. The wider estate, however, is far older, with West Dean Manor mentioned in the Domesday Book. It passed through various aristocratic hands over the centuries, until the Peachey family built the present manor in the early 1800s. The estate was then acquired by the James family in the 1890s – and passed to Edward James in 1912. But as Edward was just five years old at the time, he had to wait a couple of decades to take full charge!

It was during the 1930s and 1940s that James used his family's wealth to provide vital financial support and promotion to later A-list European artists Salvador Dali and René Magritte, as well as British creative Leonora Carrington. He also assembled one of the first – and most important – collections of Surrealism outside France, and helped spread interest in the movement to the Americas. Away from grand galleries, however, there's quiet pleasure in lapping up a quirky touch of Surrealism in the tranquil Sussex landscape. The abstract white sculpture by the trees is one of four by Eilis O'Connell on the estate.

Address West Dean, Chichester, PO18 0RX, www.westdean.ac.uk | Getting there West Dean Gardens is six miles north of Chichester via the A 286; bus 60 runs regularly from Chichester Cathedral, with a stop near the Gardens | Hours Mar–Oct Mon–Fri 10.30am–5pm, Sat & Sun 9am–4pm; Nov–Feb Mon–Fri 9.30am–4pm, Sat & Sun 9am–4pm | Tip Edward James also established an educational trust to promote arts and crafts, and since 1971 the old manor house has become West Dean College, offering a hugely popular range of creative courses taught by leading practitioners.

68__The Sweet Jar
Chewing over myriad delicious memories

Run by husband and wife team Jan and Matt Ellison, The Sweet Jar taps the power of taste memory in the same way a nibble of made-leine cakes transported the protagonist in Marcel Proust's legendary novel *À La Recherche Du Temps Perdu* back in time in an instant. 'The idea was to sell lovely sweets that take people back to their childhood,' says Jan.

The couple run two shops – one in the heart of Chichester, another in the nearby seaside resort of Bognor Regis – selling over 250 varieties of traditional sweets, fudges and rock, and when warmer weather comes, ice cream too! Customers frequently share memories of how the sweets take them back to past times with grandparents, or even World War II, when such treats were in very short supply.

The variety of flavours is dizzying. In boiled sweets, you could go for Clove Balls, Sour Sherbet Bombs or Dandelion and Burdock, while innovative flavourings in the chewy category include Watermelon Bonbons or Herbal Candy – like the Kendal mint cake beloved of mountaineers for its instant energy kick, but with extra herby buzz! There are bestsellers, though. 'We sell a huge number of aniseed balls,' says Jan. 'And people of all ages like rhubarb and custard sweets. I think it's something that's handed down to children – along with sweet peanuts, cola cubes and sherbet lemons.'

Jar labels also highlight some venerable traditional sweet makers, such as Joseph Dobson and Co – makers of things like Mega Lollies in Yorkshire since 1850 – and Welsh producer Brays, whose Newport factory has been in business since 1867. Those wanting a taste of Europe, meanwhile, can delve into continental confectionery including Dutch salt diamonds or salty herrings, Swedish cherry and chilli liquorice, Finnish cable bites, or Danish caramel and liquorice twists. And for the diet-conscious there's a pleasing range of sugar-free sweets too.

caramel

Coffee & walnut

Rhubarb

Milk chocolate

Christmas cake

Lemon cheesecake

chocolate & orange

Chocolate & mint

Seasalt caramel

Rum & raisin

Cherry & almond

Lincat

Address 18 Southgate, Chichester, PO19 1ES and 11 The Arcade, Bognor Regis, PO21 1LH, www.the-sweet-jar.co.uk | Getting there Five-minute walk from Chichester railway station | Hours Mon–Sat 10am–5.30pm | Tip If there's a traditional sweet you recall from your past, Jan is happy to turn confectionery detective to track it down – as she did with a previously requested confectionery called Toffee Crunch. And you don't have to live locally, as the shop does online orders.

69 Turner's Pies

A Sussex beacon for a British culinary classic

While other countries have pies, nowhere else has it become such an iconic food as in Britain. And nowhere else in the UK has better claim to be at the pinnacle of the British pie world than this Sussex company, whose shops now dot the region.

At the British Pie Awards – the 'Oscars' of British pie-making, held each year at an ancient church in the pork pie capital of Melton Mowbray – no other maker has won more awards. Turner's has taken the 'Pie of Pies' Supreme Champion accolade twice in the past decade, most recently the 2020 award for its Steak & Stilton Pie. The same pie also earned a place in the Guild of Fine Foods' Top 50 Foods in Britain. The company's Steak and Kidney pie, meanwhile, has twice been champion at the Pie Awards, and in 2016 Turner's pies beat hundreds of rivals in four separate categories.

It all began nearly a century ago in 1933, when Eva and Reginald Turner made a pie for a hotel in the Sussex resort of Bognor Regis. By the 1960s, Mrs Turner's steak and kidney pie had become a must-eat local treat. It was their youngest son, Pip, who set expansion going in 1985 by selling to butchers and delicatessens, and it is his three children who oversee Turner's today. They continue to invent new pies, from the 2023 bestseller Steak, Mushroom and Truffle, to vegetarian hits such as Butternut, Chilli and Cheese. Also available are seasonal pies such as the Christmas-time Turkey, Gammon and Cranberry.

Turner's original Bognor Regis pie shop opened in 1990, with the simple motto: 'Only the finest ingredients'. And although Turner's Pies are now stocked in elite outlets such as the famous food hall in London's Harrods, the company's heart and roots remain local. It was no surprise when, in 2012, the company received the Britten Trophy, awarded annually by Bognor Regis to those who have made a key contribution to the town and its community.

Address 89 Hawthorn Road, Bognor Regis, PO21 2BL; 13 East Gate Square, Chichester PO19 1JL, www.turnerspies.co.uk | **Getting there** Bognor Regis branch is 15 minutes walk from Bognor Regis railway station; train to Chichester railway station, then a 20-minute walk | **Hours** Mon–Sat 8am–4.30pm | **Tip** Beer is the perfect accompaniment to a pie, so try a range of intriguing brews at Bognor craft ale beacon The Dog & Duck (www.facebook.com/dogduckbognor).

70_ The Woolstaplers
A strange street name rooted in economic history

Today, The Woolstaplers is a short road just back from Chichester's busy West Street, but its unusual name nods to a rich trading history dating at least to the 13th century, when Chichester was one of England's key ports for wool export. In medieval times, meanwhile, the word 'staple' referred to a market place appointed by royal authority, where merchants had exclusive right of purchase of certain goods destined for export.

England's rulers made vast sums through duty on wool, as well as sheep hides plus woolfells – the traditional name for a skin from which the wool has not been sheared or pulled. A long time figure for wool duty was three pence in the (old English) pound going to the monarch. And wool-staplers were key people memorialised in the name of the street – buying wool from farmers, sorting and grading it, then selling it on to others in the business chain.

The first reference to the export of goods from Chichester is a licence given in 1226 to local merchant Emery de Rouen to ship a cargo of wool, bacon and cheese to Flanders – though historians believe such trade existed long before this date. England's monarchs frequently pledged wool tax money to pay debts, with one typical 14th-century payment going to French merchants in Aix to buy wine for the English royal court. In 1329, the customs from English wool and other exports were made over to the Bardi, an influential Florentine banking family.

For tax purposes, the area designated as the port of Chichester expanded from medieval times, eventually extending along a stretch of the English south coast from Southampton to Seaford – though rather than in the city itself, port activities were focused on Dell Quay, two miles away. Then known as La Delle, this was among the busiest ports in England. Even today, the 16th-century Crown and Anchor pub remains a popular quayside watering hole.

THE WOOLSTAPLERS

Address The Woolstaplers, Chichester, PO19 1BQ | Getting there 20-minute walk from Chichester railway station, local buses to West Street | Hours Accessible 24 hours | Tip If you feel inspired to channel your own inner wool-stapler, a great shop to buy wool is the nearby H&F Haberdashery and Fabric.

71 Blue Idol Meeting House

Birthplace of a US state – plus rare apples!

The Blue Idol was built as a farmhouse around 1580 near the medieval hamlet of Coolham – home of the Selsey Arms pub. After being used for Quaker worship for a number of years, the building was eventually bought by a group of Quaker Friends in 1691, and converted into a permanent Quaker Meeting House.

The link to America lies in that group of Friends including William Penn, who gave the US state of Pennsylvania its name – deriving from a combination of Latin words that together mean 'Penn's woods' – in honour of his father. Today's Grade II-listed house has gone through various names in its long history, including Little Slatters (the original farmhouse), Shipley Preparative Meeting and Thakeham Preparative Meeting. The main building is complemented by a barn, which is used for exhibitions. The lovely gardens that surround the house, meanwhile, are home to two ancient Quaker burial grounds. There's also a William Penn information trail.

The gardens around the Blue Idol have also played a role in preserving one of Britain's rarest apples. Known as Bossom, this historic Sussex variety was believed to be down to just a single tree, growing in the garden of a Miss Scott in the nearby village of Graffham. It was only when this tree blew down in the 1986 hurricane that grafts were hurriedly taken, and sent to the National Fruit Collection in Kent to save the variety from extinction.

By happy chance, apple hunters then found another original Bossom tree in 2020 – growing by the Blue Idol Quaker Meeting House. Again, experts were only called when the tree fell. But this time – perhaps watched over by a benign power – the tree wasn't totally uprooted. Propped up, it survived – and is now kept company by a new Bossom apple tree cultivated at the National Fruit Collection, using grafts from the lost Graffham tree.

QUAKER
AND FOUNDER
OF PENNSYLVANIA
WILLIAM PENN
1644 – 1718
WITH OTHER FRIENDS
HE ESTABLISHED THIS
MEETING HOUSE

WEST SUSSEX COUNTY COUNCIL

Address Old House Lane, Coolham, RH13 8QP, www.blueidol.org | **Getting there**
By car via the A272 between Coolham and Billingshurst (parking available), around
20 miles north-east of Chichester; Billingshurst railway station is three miles away | **Hours**
Mar–Nov Fri 10am–1pm, open for worship Sun 10.30am; its Quaker guardians are
happy to arrange group visits at other times; garden open daily during daylight hours | **Tip**
The Blue Idol Meeting House is one of 12 places on a spiritual trail, created in 2019, of
interesting religious sites around the Horsham District; see and download a trail map using
a link on the Blue Idol website: www.blueidol.org/visit.

72 Knepp Rewilding Estate
Struggling farm becomes Sussex Eden

One of the world's most inspirational wildlife conservation projects beckons 25 miles north-east of Chichester. Alongside showcasing the transformative power of a new approach to landscape management, the Knepp Rewilding Estate offers 'Safari tours', overnight wilderness stays, and a recently opened restaurant celebrating estatefarmed produce.

It's a huge change from the many years when the 3,500-acre estate was ruled by intensive farming practices, despite difficult and financially challenging soil conditions of clay over limestone. In 2001, Charlie Burrell – who took over the estate from his grandparents in 1983 – had a moment of epiphany. This was when the estate received government Countryside Stewardship funding to restore the 350-acre Repton Park at its heart, offering a chance to reimagine possibilities of use for land that had been under the plough for decades.

Burrell took particular inspiration from ideas put forward by Dutch ecologist Dr Frans Vera in his groundbreaking book *Grazing Ecology and Forest History*, which received a timely English translation in 2000. It spotlighted how large, free-roaming grazing animals – such as long-horn cattle, wild horses and pigs – could drive radical ecological change by creating a mosaic of biodiverse habitats simply from the way they trample and root the soil, snap branches and de-bark trees – all while spreading seeds and nutrients with their dung.

Today, Knepp has proven the approach in spectacular style, and the Sussex Eden has seen the return of iconic species such as beaver and storks, turtle doves, nightingales and purple emperor butterflies across its array of landscapes, from woodland to wetland. Ecological benefits – soil restoration, flood mitigation, water purification, carbon sequestration – have made it an instructive beacon for policymakers and farmers alike, as well as the lucky locals!

Address Swallows Lane, Dial Post, Horsham, RH13 8NN, www.knepp.co.uk | Getting there By car, take the A27, then the A24, and Knepp is near the village of Dial Post; bus 23 between Horsham and Worthing to Steyning Road, then a 30-minute walk | Hours Daily 7am–7pm | Tip Visit nearby Earthy Timber to browse beautiful, modern salvaged-wood furniture crafted by artist woodworker A. S. Stawicki (www.earthytimber.com).

73__The Selsey Arms
Toast war heroes against a resonant backdrop

Perched at a crossroads in the hamlet of Coolham, the décor of the 17th-century Selsey Arms pub reflects a past of smuggling, cooking and combat. Initially known as the Kings of Prussia, and then The Duke's Head, it took its current name in 1847. Stepping inside, the most striking first impression is memorabilia linked to the airbase that sprang up in nearby fields to support the 1944 D-Day landings. Operational only from April 1944 to January 1945, RAF Coolham hosted an international group of pilots, who in addition to flying sorties to attack German forces in occupied France, also chased down and destroyed Germany's V1 flying bombs before they could plunge onto England.

The airfield hosted several Polish RAF squadrons and a New Zealand one, and the pub's popularity with those aircrew is reflected not only in the wartime memorabilia, but also a simple memorial in the pub garden, which bears acknowledgement in Polish for the Poles who lost their lives flying from Coolham. Aficionados of traditional pub décor, meanwhile, should peer up at the unusual wheel with 10 segments mounted on the ceiling, with a spinner attached. Depending who you ask, this was either for playing 'twister', a game of chance that migrated to Sussex from East Anglia, or was used by the smugglers who once drank here to somehow help divide their contraband.

In addition, the space above the 1930s inglenook fireplace until recently housed an old 'dog wheel' – on which a dog would be placed to walk around like a hamster, helping cook food in the fireplace by turning a spit in the inglenook via a connecting chain! If this sounds crazy not to mention cruel, it was a cooking method that clearly had fans, as it's believed Hannah Penn – wife of local quaker William Penn, who went off to found Pennsylvania – wrote to England requesting a similar dog wheel to be sent to her in America!

Address Cowfold Road, Coolham, RH13 8QJ, www.theselseyarms.co.uk | Getting there At the junction of the A 272 and B 2139, 22 miles north-east of Chichester; train to Horsham, then bus 74 to Coolham takes just under 30 minutes | Hours Wed–Sun noon–midnight, Tue 3pm–midnight | Tip Pick up information at the pub for a heritage trail around the surrounding fields, including the 12th-century ruins of Knepp Castle, plus oak trees planted on the old site of RAF Coolham – now a farmer's field – bearing individual plaques for the airmen who died flying from here.

74 Manor Road Garage
Unexpected slice of Sussex Deco wonder

Along with its accompanying palm trees, this stunning example of Art Deco – granted Grade II-listed status by English Heritage in 2007 – seems like it should be serving folk on Miami's South Beach, rather than on a quiet street half a mile back from the Sussex coastline.

Considered of 'national importance' architecturally, the façade is a perfect example of the Deco style known as Streamline Moderne, which was added to a previously unexceptional garage opened in 1919. The extremely rare quartet of vintage Shell petrol pumps were added in the late 1940s or early 1950s. The garage operated until 1973, when its owner retired – though a clear-out found vintage Rolls Royces and an old tractor in states of disrepair inside the garage! After that the building was fenced off and left to decay for three decades.

With its curved wings, wrap-around windows and central 'fin' feature, this is a shrine to the glamour of early motoring. That air of designer luxury inspired the eventual rejuvenation of the site with the fashioning of stylish private apartments behind the stunning façade, creating a bright lounge from what was once a car showroom, whose large curved window overlooked the garage forecourt.

The Shell pumps too are gems of streamlined, curvy Modernist design, with chrome fittings adding an extra dash of cool. Peer closely, and you'll also see that each of the shell-shaped glass tops features different styles of lettering to differentiate the kind of fuel it dispensed. The desire to stand out with distinctive design saw rival fuel companies create glass globes in their own striking shapes, such as the winged ornamentation of the Cleveland company, before it became part of Esso. Fans of evocative vintage petrol pumps can find another example – for Esso – attached to a house on the High Street in the Sussex village of Handcross, 25 miles north-east.

Address Manor Road, East Preston, Littlehampton, BN16 1QA | **Getting there** 30-minute walk from Angmering railway station | **Hours** Accessible 24 hours | **Tip** Refuel with a diverse range of internationally inspired food (including American) at nearby Grub & Gumption diner (www.grubandgumption.com).

75 __ Sea Lane House

Iconic Modernist house in sleepy seaside enclave

Proof you shouldn't trust Wikipedia too much is its entry for East Preston, making no mention of this sleepy West Sussex seaside spot's claim to architectural global fame. But talk to any self-respecting modern architecture fan, and they'll certainly know of Sea Lane House. The only house in Britain designed by famed Bauhaus architect and pioneer Marcel Breuer, this beacon of 20th-century modernist domestic architecture is also his only surviving pre-World War II building in Europe, and considered the finest example of his early architecture work anywhere in the world.

Now Grade II listed, Sea Lane House was designed as a six-bedroom home, and completed in 1937. As well as familiar design tropes such as sinuous curves and a dazzling white finish, Breuer provided a key innovation by setting a projecting wing of the house on slender columns to ensure sea views from every bedroom. A graceful sun terrace juts out on another column.

Interestingly, the house was never occupied by the person by whom it was commissioned – a plantation owner called James Macnabb. Instead, it was bought in 1943 by automotive engineer Richard Papelian, noted for introducing windscreen wipers and car radios to Britain! Papelian lived in the house until his death in 1987. It remained in the family until 2012.

Born in Hungary in 1902, Breuer moved to Germany and joined the Bauhaus in the 1920s, rising to become head of its influential furniture workshop – which explains why the other famous creation in his three years in Britain was the Isokon Long Chair. Though the rise of the Nazis prompted Breuer to flee Berlin for London in 1935, he moved to the USA in 1937 to teach at Harvard. His pupils included future architecture stars Philip Johnson and I. M. Pei. Breuer's own star post-war buildings include the Whitney Museum of American Art in New York and the UNESCO Headquarters in Paris.

Address Junction Sea Lane and Gorse Avenue, Kingston Gorse Estate, East Preston, BN16 1RX | Getting there 45-minute walk from Angmering-by-Sea or Goring-by-Sea railway station | Hours Not open to the public, but the stunning exterior can be viewed from Sea Lane | Tip The nearby Bluebird Cafe offers refreshment beside a Blue Flag beach (www.thebluebirdcafeferring.co.uk).

76___Ilex Way
Hideaway arboreal avenue with Royal fans

This is another unexpected Goring jewel, though very different to the nearby Sistine Chapel reproduction! Instead, here's a magnificent 19th-century carriageway – considered among the finest examples in the world – running straight as an arrow like an arboreal take on Paris' Champs Élysées between the former villages of Goring and Ferring.

Its creation was down to the building of Goring Hall in 1840, a parkland-set manor providing grand coastal living for David Lyon, MP for a so-called 'rotten borough' – an old type of parliamentary seat for areas that had become depopulated, but remained in existence to provide positions for rich folk with no desire to actually work as MPs. Unsurprisingly, Lyon never spoke in Parliament – ironic, given that Goring Hall was designed by Charles Barry, who helped rebuild the Houses of Parliament following a devastating fire in 1834.

Lyon ordered a wide and stately mile-long avenue to provide carriage access to the Hall from both east and west, planting over 400 soaring holm oaks that have created a dramatic leafy archway along the whole length of what became known as Ilex Way, after the trees' Latin name (Quercus ilex). Walking here today, you're accompanied by a ceaseless rustle of wildlife and the sound of falling acorns. The avenue is notable as home to various species of bat, alongside myriad other plant and animal species.

Its oaks are actually Mediterranean incomers, stylish evergreens introduced in the 1500s thanks to their hardy tolerance of salty sea airs. The trees survived the urban growth all around from the 1930s onwards, though many suffered damage in the Great Storm of 1987. Plans for a mass felling saw residents form the Ilex Group to protect the trees, with key support from the late Queen Mother, whose pre-nuptial name – Elizabeth Bowes-Lyon – reflected her links to the Lyon family.

Address Ilex Way, Goring-by-Sea, BN12 4UY | **Getting there** The avenue runs between Sea Lane in Goring and Sea Lane in Ferring; the easiest point of access is a 20-minute walk south from Goring-by-Sea railway station | **Hours** Accessible 24 hours | **Tip** The Sea Lane Café is a bracing place to recharge, right beside nearby Goring beach (www.sealanecafe.co.uk).

77_Sussex's Sistine Ceiling

Startling homage to a legendary masterpiece

Of all the places you might expect to find the world's only grand scale reproduction of the Sistine Chapel ceiling, a Sussex backwater probably isn't high on the list. But here it is, hidden inside an otherwise utilitarian church on a main road in Goring-by-Sea. And its back story is a remarkable testament to devotion and obsession.

The magnificent recreation of Michelangelo's 16th-Century masterpiece of religious decoration is the creation of sign painter Gary Bevans, a local parishioner with no formal art training. His prompt came in 1987, when on a parish pilgrimage to Rome, he realised the English Martyrs Church where he worshipped shared the same proportions – two thirds the size – as the Sistine Chapel. So he did what any admiring artist might do – asked his local bishop whether he could do an epic copy of the Rome work on the church ceiling back home.

It took Bevans over five years of painstaking labour to hand-paint his Renaissance homage – about the same time Michelangelo took for the original, although Bevans was also doing his full-time sign-making job! After fixing hundreds of plywood panels to the ceiling, Bevans under-coated and primed the whole vast area, then sketched in over 500 individual figures. Detailed colour was then added, using acrylic paints that recaptured the vibrant colours brought back to the original Roman ceiling by a major restoration. The ceiling was completed in 1993, and has an advantage over the original in that it's 10 metres nearer the ground!

Bevans' creation was the subject of a 2008 documentary, plus coverage by TV channels from the UK, US, Australia, New Zealand and Japan, and the project has been being highlighted in *Time* magazine. The Vatican demonstrated its approval of his unique artistic tribute by awarding Bevans the papal cross *Pro Ecclesia et Pontifical*. Despite this, Bevans continues his sign-writing work.

Address English Martyrs Church, Goring Way, Goring-by-Sea, BN12 4UH, www.english-martyrs.co.uk | Getting there 10-minute walk from Goring-by-Sea railway station (30 minutes from Chichester); 18 miles east of Chichester via the A27 then the A259 | Hours Mon 10am–1pm, Tue–Fri 10am–4pm | Tip Be sure to buy the £1 leaflet pack that provides a wealth of detail about Bevans' other paintings around the church, including an homage to Leonardo's *The Last Supper*, which includes two intriguing figures in modern dress alongside Jesus.

78 Itchenor Boat Trips

Ancient ferry meets 21st-century pioneer

However beautiful its waters and banks, Chichester Harbour's 50-plus miles of shore is a barrier if you don't have a boat. Step forward the little Itchenor Ferry, established in the 17th century to bear travellers across a few hundred metres of water between Bosham Hoe Hard and the pretty village of Itchenor – otherwise, a distance of 13 miles on foot!

The ferry operated 24 hours a day for nearly four centuries until waning demand saw it discontinued in 1964. The pause in its historic service was temporary, however, and in 1976 the ferry was reintroduced by Chichester Harbour Conservancy as a pleasing link in the local footpath network.

The Solar Heritage catamaran provides a unique 21st-century contrast. As the name suggests, it uses sun power for its eco-friendly progress around inlets and tidal mudflats on regular wildlife and history tours. As well as zero emissions plus silent running that minimises disturbance to wildlife, its twin hulls minimise shoreline erosion caused by the wash of engined boats. Regular Harbour Discovery and Wildlife Explorer trips give passengers the opportunity to spot seals, as well as a wonderful array of birdlife, plus evocative landmarks such as Bosham Church (the only church to feature on the 11th-century Bayeux Tapestry) and the remains of an Iron Age salt works.

Though it has plied Chichester Harbour since 2004, the boat began life as one of a trio of solar ferries carrying art lovers to view giant installations set into the water of Switzerland's Three Lakes region as part of the Swiss 2002 National Exposition. Picking up on the Exposition theme of Alternative Energy, Chichester Harbour Conservancy obtained one of the boats to inspire local awareness of the subject. And don't worry about the effects of cloudy weather: so effective are Solar Heritage's panels that it can generate charge even from moonlight!

Address Ferry: Itchenor Jetty, The Street, Itchenor, Chichester, PO20 7AW, www.itchenorferry.co.uk; Solar Heritage: www.conservancy.co.uk | Getting there By car, take the A 286 south signposted Witterings, then the B 2179, then turn on to Itchenor Road just after Russell's Garden Centre; bus 52 to Russell's Garden Centre, then a 30-minute walk | Hours Itchenor Ferry: May–Sep daily 9am–6pm; Apr & Oct Sat & Sun 9am–6pm; Nov Sat & Sun 10am–4pm; Solar Heritage all year round (see website for details) | Tip At the end of an alley by Itchenor Quay, the Quarterdeck Cafe offers drinks, ice creams and light meals amid yachts perched on shore for shipyard attention (www.quarterdeckcafe.co.uk).

79 Bailiffscourt Hotel

Unique homage to medieval luxury

Down a lane in an unspoilt coastal hinterland is what seems a sumptuous ancient manor wrapped in a tranquil estate stretching back from the golden sand and dunes of Climping Beach. But Bailiffscourt has a quirky secret: despite ravishing appearances, it didn't exist until the late 1920s.

The house was designed for Jazz Era aristocrat Lord Moyne – Walter Guinness of the famous brewing family – who bought the 750-acre estate on which the hotel stands in the 1920s to block the building of a housing estate around the family's not-so-grand seaside holiday home – which also protected one of the largest stretches of undeveloped coast in West Sussex.

At the time, the site was home to just a modest farmhouse and the 13th-century chapel that still stands. When Lord Moyne decided to build a manor house befitting the estate he had unexpectedly acquired, he demanded it be built not just in the medieval style his wife Evelyn loved, but from original materials. To fulfil this ambitious recreation, architect Amyas Phillips scoured the country for appropriate ancient stone, woodwork, doors, windows and fireplaces. The soaring roof beams in one bedroom, for example, once propped up a centuries-old barn.

Completed in 1935, Bailiffscourt was briefly a beacon for 1930s high society until the death of Lady Moyne in 1939, just before the outbreak of World War II, when the family left the house. The 1944 assassination of Lord Moyne in Palestine meant they never returned. The house became a hotel in 1948, and has since 1993 been owned by Historic Sussex Hotels. They have burnished Bailiffscourt's medieval template, creating an interior adorned with aged furniture, draped with ravishing tapestries, lit through Gothic windows. Come for a stay or spa treat, explore the parkland or secluded beach, or just enjoy this glorious tribute to medieval style over tea or a meal.

Address Climping Street, Atherington, Littlehampton, BN17 5RW, www.hshotels.co.uk/bailiffscourt | Getting there By car via the A 259 between Littlehampton and Bognor Regis | Hours Accessible 24 hours | Tip Bailiffscourt has a sister hotel – The Spread Eagle – fashioned from a genuine 15th-century inn, 20 miles away in Midhurst (www.hshotels.co.uk/spread-eagle).

80 Creative Heart
Distinctive community hub making a difference

Creative Heart is a welcoming community hub and arts café in the heart of Littlehampton, working to tackle social isolation and loneliness by bringing people together through a range of activities – as well as simply providing a cosy space for anyone to drop in to eat, drink and chat under the slogan 'Creating community, creating change'. This fine initiative is overseen by three inspiring women: Claire Jones, Fliss Jay and Mary Acland.

Fliss and Claire had run a community craft group called Cre8 in Littlehampton for many years, and always dreamed of creating a larger community hub with its own permanent space. Mary, meanwhile, had collaborated with Fliss and Claire on retreats and events, as well as being an active member of other community organisations around Littlehampton.

The café side of the operation is based on a menu of homely, locally sourced food for delicious salad bowls and other offerings, and a similar admirable ethos percolates through other aspects of Creative Heart's community offering. The space is decorated using upcycled, reclaimed and second-hand furniture, and there is a wider effort to choose sustainable, ethical and local options wherever possible – including avoiding single use plastics. Composting and recycling are woven into the operation to avoid unnecessary waste.

Alongside creative art and craft classes, free activities run at Creative Heart include Men's Talk Time in the café, Wed Writers club, Knit and Natter sessions, a digital workshop – and even beginners' bass guitar lessons! One of the most inspiring initiatives, however, is a weekly Veterans Peer Support group, which provides an opportunity for military veterans and their families to meet together over a drink to chat about some of the specific issues that can affect service personnel – such as trauma – as well as getting advice on help available.

Address 42 Beach Road, Littlehampton, BN17 5HT, www.creativeheart.org.uk | Getting there 20-minute walk from Littlehampton railway station | Hours Tue–Sat 9.30am–4pm | Tip As a striking artistic complement to Creative Heart's veteran support work, 100 metres away at Caffyns Field, by the Littlehampton War Memorial, is a poignant wooden chainsaw sculpture by Simon Groves of a lone soldier from World War I.

81 East Beach Cafe

Eye-popping piece of nature-inspired architecture

When Littlehampton resident Jane Wood purchased the site of what is now the East Beach Cafe, she did so only as a desperate way to stop the planned development of a two-storey edifice that would have ruined her sea view. So she found herself with a prime seafront plot, but no idea what to do with it… Enter Fate via a chance meeting with now A-list architect designer Thomas Heatherwick at a charity lunch. The result of their chat is one of Sussex's most striking buildings, voted by the Royal Institute of British Architects among the star UK constructions of 2007.

What Heatherwick came up with for what was his first British building was an architectural wonder inspired by a warped, mottled hunk of weathered driftwood. 'The seaside at Littlehampton has a raw beauty,' enthused Heatherwick at the time. 'Rather than make something swanky and shiny, we decided to make something that almost looks like it's from the sea.'

Rather than straight edges and right angles, the East Beach Cafe is a rippling shell made from sliced metal sections forged in a specialist Littlehampton foundry known to Heatherwick from other projects. Each section was rusted with seawater to provide a suitably weathered coastal patina then, after nine months of crafting, lifted into place one sunny morning, with prayers that this complex piece of engineering would slot together – which it did perfectly.

Today, it's a seafront beacon contrasting brilliantly with more old-fashioned seaside charms around, such as ice cream or fish and chip kiosks, amusement arcades and crazy golf. A wide glass frontage opens to adjacent beach and ocean. Inside, a pale dining space mirrors the ripples of the outside, managing to be both cutting edge and cosy, like the inside of some slightly surreal cave. A stroll along the seafront promenade lets you reflect on how even star architects have to start somewhere.

Address The Promenade, Littlehampton, BN17 5GB, www.eastbeachcafe.co.uk | Getting there 30-minute walk from Littlehampton railway station | Hours Daily 10am–4pm, Fri & Sat also 5.30–9pm | Tip West Beach Cafe is the East Beach's simpler but still elegant and modern waterside cousin, designed by Asif Khan – the man behind the 2012 Olympics Beat Box Pavilion – on the west bank of the River Arun where it meets the sea. Cross the river via the pedestrian bridge a few hundred metres inland then walk to the river mouth (www.facebook.com/westbeachcafe1).

82__East Pier Lighthouse
Reminder of war – and sibling light makers

Today's East Pier Lighthouse rises like a cross between a mid-century abstract construction and an escapee from a science fiction vision of the future – a white 7-metre concrete tower whose cylindrical lantern perches at the top of four gracefully tapering buttresses at the western end of Littlehampton's shingly town beach, where it meets the mouth of the Arun River.

Built in 1948, this eye-catching edifice replaced two hexagonal light towers that were put here in Victorian times. The first was built in 1848 and stood 40 feet tall (13 metres), while its companion appeared in 1868 and stood 26 feet tall (8 metres). Built in wood with green-domed roofs, the pair of lights became affectionately known as the Salt and Pepper Pots, and projected their light seven miles out into the English Channel. Despite their decades of fine service, World War II saw the two Victorian beacons deliberately demolished in 1940 to prevent enemy forces using them as navigational markers – leaving mariners off this shore to be on extra guard for the next eight years.

The story behind the lenses used in the historic lighthouses, meanwhile, shines a light on impressive brotherly achievement. In 1824, the Chance brothers – Lucas and William – set up an eponymous glassworks in the West Midlands to produce hi-spec lenses for lighthouses. The firm became a pioneer in glass technology, whose renown means that today Chance lenses remain in over 2,500 lighthouses around the world. The company, however, is now based in Australia.

For the technically minded, the lighthouse features a 4th order Chance fixed lens produced in 1869, which shines in a 6 seconds on, 1.5 seconds off pattern. It shows a white light over the English channel to the south/south-east and yellow towards the south/south-west. Nearby benches provide a seafront spot for watching the play of light on the waves as evening approaches.

Address Beach end of Pier Road, Littlehampton, BN17 5LR | Getting there 25-minute walk from Littlehampton railway station | Hours Accessible 24 hours | Tip The RNLI lifeboat station, just a few hundred metres inland from the lighthouse, offers distinctive gifts that help support safety at sea.

83__Gaugemaster

Get on the right track in miniature style

The list of superstar model train set enthusiasts includes Rod Stewart, Elton John, Neil Young and Tom Hanks. Frank Sinatra loved them too. And here is a model world headline act in its own right, drawing fans to the quiet Sussex station at Ford, beside a curve of the river Arun.

Describing itself as 'The Model Shop for Big Imaginations', this beacon of adult playfulness is the result of the shunting together of a model shop (The Engine Shed) and electronic controller company Gaugemaster, relocating from other places in 1988 to buy the disused Station Goods Yard at Ford station. They opened a year later, and have since gone from strength to strength, with Open Weekend showcases attracting up to 4,000 people.

Now one of the largest model shops in the UK, there are over 20,000 products in stock – including some that whizz around the shop to entertain customers. As well as train-related kit, model car fans are catered for too, with everything from racing Scalextric to metal models from classic companies such as Dinky. Aircraft fans, meanwhile, can snap up accurate scale versions of classic planes from World War II legends to modern jets. As well as iconic British modelling names such as Airfix and Humbrol, the shop is also a prime source for a host of otherwise hard-to-find international brands including Atlas, Kato, Kestrel and NSR. It's also the sole UK distributor of renowned European brands Roco and Fleischmann. All these complement the shop's own-brand Gaugemaster Collection.

You'll be impressed, too, by the expansive range of products needed to create your own miniature railway system. Check out an array of 'scenic products' such as trackside trees, station flower beds and flocks of sheep, as well as various sets of passengers and railway personnel. Sadly, the traditionally-dressed porters are no longer available at real-life British stations to help with baggage.

Address Gaugemaster House, Ford Road, Ford, Arundel, BN18 0BN,
www.gaugemaster.com | **Getting there** Beside Ford railway station | **Hours** Mon–Sat
9am–5.30pm, Sun 10.30am–3.30pm | **Tip** Ride on beautiful miniature trains at Amberley
Museum, with its array of characterful, vintage narrow gauge trains, including classic steam
engines (www.amberleynarrowgauge.co.uk).

84__The Long Bench

Take a seat on a multicoloured meandering marvel

Stretching for 324 metres along the seafront promenade at Little-hampton is the longest bench in Britain – and one of the longest in the world. The wood and stainless steel bench takes a flowing form that curves around lamp posts and obstacles, dropping down to paths, and piling up into helter skelter shapes in a series of striking sea-front shelters.

The bench was opened in July 2010 and can seat over 300 people. It was funded by Arun District Council and the UK's 'Sea Change' capital grants programme for cultural and creative regeneration in seaside resorts. The structure was designed by Studio Weave with the help of local school children, and further funding came from Gordon Roddick as a tribute to his late wife Anita – founder of the global Body Shop cosmetics chain, which first began trading in Littlehampton, where it still has its HQ.

The thousands of slats that make up the Long Bench are formed from salvaged tropical hardwood harvested from a variety of species. This diversity offers wood of different shades, which is augmented by steel bars in myriad colours which are incorporated into the bench at different spots where it weaves and plummets. Over 200 of the slats are engraved with messages and memories from visitors and local people, and anyone can add one of their own to the bench by visiting the Long Bench website (www.longbench.org). As an ever-evolving project, the bench's personalised slats remain in place for five years before being replaced by others engraved with new memories and messages.

Some of the slats are made of recycled reddish brown hardwood from a particularly impressive African tree species known as sapele. Growing up to 45 metres high, this wood is harder than mahogany. Naturally, all sapele used in the Long Bench is from sustainably managed sources, before each slat is sanded and engraved in local charity workshops.

Address Eastern Promenade, Littlehampton, BN17 5GB | Getting there 20-minute walk from Littlehampton railway station | Hours Accessible 24 hours | Tip The slat-making workshops are at Aldingbourne Country Centre, run by a charity helping people with learning disabilities or autism to live independent lives. The Centre also has an open farm, woodland walks and other attractions (www.aldingbournecountrycentre.org).

85 — Oyster Waymarkers

Riverside cookery lessons in metal and stone

Installed in 2007, this set of six waymarkers stretches along the River Walkway in Littlehampton, providing a culinary reflection on the town's relationship with the sea. It makes a special nod to the historical Oyster Pond created at the seaward end of the promenade in the late 18th century to store the succulent bivalves brought ashore at the time as part of a flourishing shellfish trade.

Fashioned from granite and metal, each waymarker consists of a low column with a circular plaque on top, every one inscribed with a different seafood recipe. The outer edge of each plaque is decorated with a large oyster shell motif. The recipes have been written with incised letters so that hungry passersby can take rubbings onto paper rather than just a snap on their phone – creating a printed recipe to take away, as well as providing an old-fashioned fun activity.

This sense of active engagement chimes with how the waymarkers were created by sculptors Brian Fell and Gordon Young, who teamed up with pupils at Littlehampton Community School. Working with the children, the artists cooked diverse local seafoods to come up with the recipes, complemented by drawings, poems and other work from the children. The mysteriously named dish of Hampton Oysters suggests grilling the shellfish with spring onion and melted cheese, while other recipes feature huss, mackerel, bass and pollack.

Though created to store oysters, by the early 20th century the Oyster Pond had become popular with children as a boating lake for their toy ships – a fact celebrated by events such as a model boating regatta held there in 1912.

The project was part of a wider initiative funded by local and national arts organisations to encourage regeneration in Littlehampton, plus the neighbouring resort of Bognor Regis, where new decorative railings were installed at a weather station opposite the Pier. A great place to eat seafood nearby is 47 Mussel Row on Pier Road.

GRILLED PLAICE

PLAICE CLEANED, DARK SKIN REMOVED
100G MELTED BUTTER

1. PREHEAT GRILL
2. PLACE FISH ON A GREASED BAKING TRAY SKIN
SIDE DOWN
3. BRUSH WITH MELTED BUTTER
4. GRILL BOTH SIDES UNTIL GOLDEN BROWN
TAKE CARE WHEN TURNING THE FISH

SERVE

Address Pier Road/Arun Parade, Littlehampton, BN17 | Getting there 10-minute
walk from Littlehampton railway station | Hours Accessible 24 hours | Tip You
can see a beautiful painting by Sydney Pike which evocatively captures fishing life
in 19th-century Littlehampton at the Littlehampton Museum on Church Street
(www.littlehamptonmuseum.co.uk).

86 Cowdray Ruins

Haunted reminder of a glorious past

Set in the Saxon town of Midhurst by the liquid thread of the River Rother, amid a vast South Downs estate, Cowdray was once one of England's most important early Tudor houses. An aristocratic manor had, however, stood here since the 13th century, taking the name 'Coudraie' from the Norman French word for a nearby hazel wood. Illustrious past guests included both Elizabeth I and Henry VIII, who stayed here with Catherine Parr. Guy Fawkes, the most famous of the plotters who tried to blow up the Houses of Parliament in 1605, also worked here.

The ruins we see today are what remain of the house built in the early 16th century. But disaster struck one evening in 1793 when, during redecoration works, it's believed smouldering charcoal in a carpenter's workshop set wood shavings alight. The blaze left only the kitchen tower intact, containing a Tudor kitchen which can occasionally be visited. Restoration work carried out over 1909–1914 is credited with saving the ruins from total collapse.

Rather than misfortune, some blame an ancient curse for various tragedies that struck the house and its residents. Legend claims an enraged monk confronted Cowdray's 16th-century owner Sir Anthony Brown, and cursed him for accepting sanctified land (including nearby Easebourne Priory) following Henry VIII's dissolution of the monasteries. The monk's hex on Sir Antony allegedly promised that 'By fire and water thy line shall come to an end'.

Any curse seems to have been on a long timer, though, as bad events didn't begin to happen for over two centuries. Within days of the 1793 fire, however, Lord Montague drowned on the River Rhine in Germany, still unaware that his house had been destroyed. When the house passed to his sister, her sons then drowned off Bognor in 1815. The ghost of Lady Montague also still reputedly stalks the burned-out shell of her former home.

Address Cowdray Heritage Trust, Midhurst, GU29 9AL, www.cowdray.co.uk | Getting there Midhurst is 12 miles north of Chichester via the A286; bus 60 runs from Chichester Cathedral to Midhurst, taking around 45 minutes; the ruins are accessed by a path beside Midhurst bus station at the top of North Street | Hours Accessible 24 hours | Tip Fitzcanes Café at the top of North Street is a beacon of vegan baking and locally made ice-cream, where industrial furniture and art works provide a lovely retro vibe (www.fitzcanes.com).

87 Glasshouse at Woolbeding

An architectural jewel reflecting on plant history

Set on the edge of historic National Trust gardens, this 21st-century re-imagining of a glasshouse is in its way as striking as the futuristic aerial gardens of Singapore, described by its renowned architect creator, Thomas Heatherwick, as 'an object that starts like a jewel and ends like a crown'.

This Glasshouse has a life of its own. It consists of a 10-sided structure made up of giant glass and metal 'sepals' – the outer, leafy plant elements that protect flowers in bud – which unfold slowly over several minutes in warm weather, opening into a giant flattened crown to allow fresh air and sunlight to reach the sub-tropical plants within.

Its inspiration is the fabled Silk Route, which for centuries saw a flow of exotic trade – and iconic plants – from the Middle East and Asia to Europe. A Silk Route Garden frames the Glasshouse, giving visitors a living journey through history, with stories of how plants such as rosemary, lavender and fennel were borne across rugged mountains, deserts and high pastures, to arrive in Britain for the adornment of both dining tables and gardens.

Other notable plants among over 300 species spread through a dozen sections are fragrant Gallica roses, originating in ancient Persia, and a rare example of *Aralia vietnamensis*, which provides shade for lush ferns alongside umbrella trees, magnolias and bananas.

Though created using modern engineering technology, the Glasshouse also draws on the history of Victorian ornamental terrariums to provide a remarkable jewel-like focal point to what 19th-century British Prime Minister Benjamin Disraeli called 'the loveliest valley in the land'. It also provides a futuristic complement to two other outstanding creations at Woolbeding – William Pye's glorious water sculpture and Philip Jebb's Neoclassical folly, each created as monuments to magnificent fallen trees.

Address Brambling Lane, Woolbeding, Midhurst, GU29 9RR, www.nationaltrust.org.uk |
Getting there Visitors travelling by car must take a National Trust minibus departing
regularly throughout the day from a collection point at Grange Centre car park, Bepton
Road, Midhurst GU29 9HD; bus 60 runs regularly from Chichester to Midhurst | Hours
Open during spring and summer; see website for details | Tip Around four miles west of
Woolbeding Gardens, the ancient St George's Church at Trotton is home to some of the
finest medieval wall paintings in England.

88__Iping Common

Come for dazzling heather, stay for the stars

One of southern England's finest areas of lowland heath, Iping Common offers a natural wonderland just west of Midhurst. Overseen by Sussex Wildlife Trust, its 125 hectares are home to distinctive species, and some of the loveliest views in the South Downs National Park. It's also one of England's best places to see the Milky Way at night.

Over 80 per cent of lowland heath has been lost from the UK over the last two centuries, and with the UK being home to a fifth of the global expanse of this remarkable ecosystem, this makes lowland heath rarer than tropical rainforests. As well as the area's distinctive dry acidic soils, the common boasts ponds, woods and grassland. A programme including controlled burning, managed by the Sussex Wildlife Trust, has helped boost the growth of expanses of the brightly coloured heather for which Iping Common is particularly renowned.

Heathland birds such as nightjar, tree pipit and woodlark nest here at ground level, the latter filling the air with melancholy song. With such key ground-nesting species, please note that dogs must be kept on a short leash. Other avian stars include the Dartford warbler, now found only in rare spots such as this. In summer, tiny silver-studded blue butterflies flutter over the bell heather, part of a complex interplay of existence with local ants, which take the butterfly caterpillars into their subterranean nests, and care for them in exchange for a sugary excretion.

There's resonant human history too, with barrows – burial mounds dating to the Bronze Age – dotting the common. One, located around 200 metres northwest of Fitzhall Lodge, is complemented by a stretch of Roman road that cuts across what is today known as the Greensand Ridge. Add a literary link, with Iping village claiming to be the setting for H. G. Wells' famous story *The Invisible Man* – although nearby South Harting makes that claim too!

Address Iping Common car park, Elsted Road, Midhurst, GU29 0PB,
www.sussexwildlifetrust.co.uk | Getting there By car, head west out of Midhurst via the
A 272, take the third turn on the left towards Elsted, and the car park is a quarter of a mile
on the right | Hours Accessible 24 hours | Tip The GoStargazing website has a dedicated
page offering detailed astronomy insights into what you might see gazing up from Iping
Common: www.gostargazing.co.uk.

89 Midhurst Museum

Pint-sized showcase of a retro cornucopia

If you'd wandered along the quirkily named Knockhundred Row a few decades ago, you'd have found fashion, antiques and books being sold in and around a 16th-century timbered building that housed Knockhundred Market. Now those are among the things providing evocative memories at a diminutive museum, which at one point claimed to be the smallest in the world.

What is today the charming Midhurst Museum opened in 2011 in the old entrance of the former market, occupying an area just under three metres square. In this tiny space, a team of volunteers initially showcased small selections of items gathered by local historian brothers Dave and Tim Rudwick, changing the theme every month. And there was plenty to choose from, as the brothers had quickly gone from traditional collectables such as coins and stamps, to gathering a wonderfully diverse range of other items. These provided material for exhibitions covering topics as different as equestrianism, Georgian Midhurst and the emergency services!

Since then, the Museum has expanded into other of the old market spaces, creating small permanent displays chronicling Midhurst from the Stone Age to the 20th century. For many, though, it's the retro mementoes in the upstairs room that strike the most resonant chord: vintage fashion, advertising and toys, plus oddities including eye-popping 19th-century vacuum cleaners!

A downstairs room is stuffed with publications delving deeper into the history of the area, including intriguing topics such as Midhurst's ties to visionary author H. G. Wells. A blue plaque on the nearby Midhurst Grammar School records his often troubled time there as both a pupil and, briefly, a reluctant teacher.

The Knockhundred name, meanwhile, may derive from an ancient land division known as a 'Hundred', one theory being that authorities could 'knock up' 100 men along this street to combat an enemy.

Address 7–8 Knockhundred Row, Midhurst, GU29 9DQ,
www.midhurstmuseumandtearooms.co.uk | Getting there Midhurst is 12 miles north of
Chichester via the A286; bus 60 runs regularly from Chichester Cathedral to Midhurst,
stopping on the adjacent North Street | Hours Tue–Sat 10.30am–4pm | Tip Visitors
looking for historic objects they can take away should browse the antiques outlets clustered
together on nearby West Street.

90 Horse Guards Inn
Historic, quirky gastropub

Hidden away in the hamlet of Tillington at the western edge of the vast Petworth Estate is a distinctive 350-year-old inn that has garnered justified national acclaim – including beating over 5,000 rivals to be chosen as the UK's Pub of the Year by the *Good Pub Guide* in 2017.

The Horse Guards got its name in the 1840s, when it was a popular watering hole for cavalry soldiers enjoying drinks and vittles while their horses grazed at Petworth. Today's patrons come from near and far to enjoy an outstanding menu majoring on ingredients widely sourced from Sussex producers, foraged from surrounding fields and hedgerows, or dug fresh from the Inn's kitchen garden. Think South Downs venison, Rye scallops and Selsey prawns, alongside homemade Sussex dairy ice-cream. Even the rapeseed oil is local.

But what sets the Horse Guards apart from countless other fine gastropubs is the charmingly distinctive spaces it serves up alongside outstanding food. Against a classic woody backdrop of distressed floor boards, uneven beams and old pine tables, husband-and-wife owners Sam and Mischa Beard dot their rambling collection of rooms with a constantly changing array of decorative curiosities, from flower-draped taxidermy to eye-catching vintage prints.

A large back garden continues the fun, providing a relaxed and characterful *al fresco* dining area, with rustic antique furniture scattered around the grass and trees, while a diverse range of colourful chickens wander contentedly among the tables and chairs – including a few hay bale seats.

While the garden beckons when the sun is shining, in winter visitors can huddle cosily inside to roast foraged chestnuts on one of several crackling log fires, or enjoy a board game scooped from the bar. If you want to stay longer, there are three upmarket bedrooms: two upstairs in the pub, another in an adjacent cottage.

Address Upperton Road, Tillington, Petworth, GU28 9AF, www.thehorseguardsinn.co.uk |
Getting there By car via A 272, around three miles west of Petworth | **Hours** Bar open
Wed–Sun 11am–11pm; kitchen Wed–Sat noon–2.30pm & 6–9pm, Sun noon–4pm | **Tip**
Take time to admire the 'Scots Crown' architectural topping of the spire of All Hallows church
just across the road; you'll be in good company, as both of England's most famous 19th-century
artists – J. M. W. Turner and John Constable – visited Tillington to capture it in paint.

91 Newlands House Gallery

Modern art set against a gorgeous Georgian backdrop

Carved from a Georgian townhouse, Newlands House has turned an 18th-century building in the heart of Petworth into a striking and intimate complement to the art treasures by Turner and others at nearby Petworth House. Since opening in 2020 with a tribute to photographer Helmut Newton, its dozen rooms have showcased some of the world's greatest creatives of the past century, ranging from designers such as Ron Arad to visual artists as varied as Joan Miró, Sean Scully, Julian Opie and Frank Auerbach.

Curator Maya Binkin spoke to Petworth Places in 2022 about the distinctive task of staging exhibitions in a 200-year-old house: 'We have become so accustomed to 'white cube' spaces or the grand halls of big museums, that it is really stimulating to see art in a domestic environment,' she said. For her, the joy of Newlands House Gallery is its combination of generously proportioned Georgian rooms, complemented by owner Nicola Jones' decision to retain original features such as the fireplaces and decorative mouldings. 'It makes my job more challenging, but the experience for our audiences is unrivalled,' said Binkin.

One of the most recent shows featured a magnificent presentation of over 90 black-and-white and colour photographs by Eve Arnold, ranging from iconic images of film stars such as Marilyn Monroe to rarely seen visuals of fashion shows in New York's Harlem in the 1950s. Some of the images were on view for the first time in 70 years.

Alongside books and postcards, the gallery shop also offers prints of works that have been exhibited, such as the photographs of Lee Miller – as well as limited edition prints by artists such as Sean Scully. Newlands House attracts visitors from across the UK, following a strategy Maya Binkin describes simply as making shows by exciting artists and presenting their works in refreshing ways.

Address Newlands House, Pound Street, Petworth, GU28 0DX,
www.newlandshouse.gallery | **Getting there** Petworth is around 14 miles north of Chichester
via the A 283; bus 99 runs from central Chichester; train to Pulborough railway station, then
a 5-mile taxi ride | **Hours** Wed–Sat 10am–5pm, Sun 11am–4pm | **Tip** E-Street Bar &
Grill offers a fine place to eat just a stone's throw from Newlands House. Decorated with
Art Deco touches, it also has a wine list highlighting several award-winning local Sussex
vineyards (www.estreetbarandgrill.co.uk).

92 Old Railway Hotel

Classic comfort in captivating choo-choos

This former Victorian railway station provides one of Britain's most distinctive places to stay – or just enjoy afternoon tea. As well as the old station house – stylishly restored in bright Nordic style – guests can bed down in luxurious 1910s/20s carriages arrayed along the old platform. Dating back over a century, each oozes retro glamour, with dark panelling, sleek wooden shutters, antique furniture and vintage travel posters.

Petworth began welcoming trains in 1859, but today's station building was constructed in 1892, and owes its rather grand style to being the stepping off point for high society travellers coming down from London to attend racing and other upper class activities at nearby Goodwood. Passengers arriving here included the future Edward VII.

Without that draw, it's possible that no station would have been built here at all, due to the poverty of the area. Reporting on the arrival of trains, the *West Sussex Gazette* went so far as to compare the area around the new station to 'the backwoods of America'. As an example of lack of worldliness, the paper noted how local inhabitants were apparently frightened by their first glimpse of a steam engine.

With the rise of motor car ownership after World War II, rail travel declined, and eventually the decision was made to close Petworth station for passenger services in 1955, though freight ran until 1966. Its rebirth in 1995 as a place to stay began with two rooms in the Station House, followed in 1998 by the arrival of the first two Pullman carriages: Mimosa (dating to 1914) and Alicante (1912). Two further carriages – Flora and Montana (both 1923) – now sit by a long platform dotted with tables and chairs for breakfast and afternoon teas, as well as a Classical-style statue. Future plans envisage creating a faithful copy of the old station signal box to provide yet another memorable room.

Address Station Road, Petworth, GU28 0JF, www.old-station.co.uk | **Getting there** 2 miles south of Petworth on the A 285 towards Chichester | **Hours** Hotel check-in 3–6pm; afternoon tea 1.30–4.30pm | **Tip** Right next door to the Old Railway Hotel, take time to drop into Badgers. Established in the late 1800s as The Railway Inn, it provided the old charabanc stop for travellers on their way to Goodwood racecourse, as well as serving arrivals at Petworth station. Full of period charm, it offers a different immersion in history, as well as good food and drink (www.badgerspetworth.co.uk).

93 Petworth Antiques
One of Britain's vintage design meccas

Whilst the grand 17th-century Petworth House and its vast country estate dominate the eponymous Sussex village in many minds, Petworth also stands out as the only town outside London to boast over 30 arts and antiques dealers within a one mile radius. There are, in fact, around 70 dealers selling wonderfully contrasting wares around the ancient streets of its compact centre.

Across the road from the Church of St Mary the Virgin, for example, Phoenix Antiques has a cornucopia of temptations including vintage cameras, old apothecary bottles and Deco pottery. That miscellany contrasts with the offerings next door at John Bird, whose focus on older times mingles antique garden paraphernalia with 18th-century medicine drawers. Petworth's antique spots handily cluster a stone's throw from each other on adjacent short streets, throwing up more enticing contrasts, such as silverware-and-clocks specialist Chequers contrasting with Mid Century Modern beacon BEAR on New Street.

On the High Street, Dickson Rendall offers what Lesley Rendall describes as 'top-end 20th-century European design', while across the road there are fabulous old posters and other printed paraphernalia at J Giles. Next door, vintage fashion accessories at Bradley's Past & Present offer something retro and stylish to wear at the Goodwood Revival vintage festival held every August.

Around 40 dealers come together at Petworth Antiques Market, where you might find 19th-century skittles alongside an Art Deco cocktail kit. 'We try to be all-inclusive with stock ranging across all eras, back to the 16th century,' says owner Kathryn Mandry. They also have a fine selection of antique copper cookware that echoes the vast array on show in the Petworth House kitchen. 'But you can buy things here that you can't touch there!' she adds. Or wear, in the case of the striking Deco-era ring bought here on a recent visit.

Address Most shops cluster along High Street, Lombard Street and East Street, www.discoverpetworth.uk | **Getting there** By car, Petworth sits at the crossroads of the A283 and A272; train to Pulborough railway station, then a 5-mile taxi ride; bus 99 from Chichester | **Hours** Vary from shop to shop | **Tip** Just over a mile from Petworth, Coultershaw Beam Pump (www.coultershaw.co.uk) is a working waterwheel that still powers an 18th-century beam pump in an enchanting riverside setting. An exhibition explains the history of Coultershaw, and its early use of water power.

94 Petworth Cottage Museum
Looking glass into a forgotten world

Petworth Cottage Museum was once a worker's cottage owned by the Leconfield Estate – the private estate centred on the grand 17th-century Petworth House. It offers a glimpse into the lives of ordinary workers that contrasts with the usual focus on the aristocratic denizens of the English country house they serviced.

The cottage has been restored as it might have been around 1910. At that time the occupier was an Irish Catholic seamstress called Mary Cummings. She was married to farrier Michael Thomas Cummings, who also worked at Petworth House. Their 17th-century cottage was originally a timber-framed building, and was part of a larger house, which was divided into two dwellings and sold to the Leconfield Estate in 1854.

The living room contains a coal-fired range – usually alight whenever the museum is open, as it would have been in the past, to provide for cooking and hot water. The table is set for tea, and all the food is real. Reflecting Mary's occupation, one room is set up as a sewing room, with a treadle sewing machine from the 1890s – surrounded by materials and fashions of that era. Decoration was aided by a collection of Edwardian photographs of Petworth cottage interiors. The period wallpaper was sourced from the reconstructed historic village of Beamish in the north of England, while local people generously gave objects, furniture and fabrics known to have been part of a household in that era. Tests revealed the upper floor walls in 1910 to have been painted a subtle green, which was copied by upmarket paint company Farrow & Ball then marketed as Petworth Green.

Additional research also found photographs of Mary Cummings' husband, as well as her son – wonderfully named Saint Michaelangelo – but, alas, no pictures of Mary herself. She lived in the cottage until 1930, when she moved to a nearby almshouse, where she died in 1935.

Address 346 High Street, Petworth, GU28 0AU, www.petworthcottagemuseum.co.uk |
Getting there Petworth is 15 miles north of Chichester via the A 285; bus 99 runs between
Chichester and Petworth | Hours 1 Apr–31 Oct Tue–Sat 2–4.30pm | Tip If you want
to see where Mary Cummings is buried, she – and her mother, plus her son Alfred – lie in
the graveyard at St Anthony and St George Roman Catholic church at Duncton, on the
A 285 three miles south of Petworth.

95 Petworth House North Gallery

Two Earls' passion for art

The painter John Constable famously called Petworth 'that House of Art'. In its long history, two men shaped its interiors and collections more than anyone else: Charles Wyndham, 2nd Earl of Egremont (1710–1763) and his son, George O'Brien Wyndham (1751–1837). Charles had been on a 'Grand Tour' of Italy, where he had acquired an array of antique sculptures, for which, between 1754 and 1763, he built a special gallery at the north end of the house, lit by large windows.

George, 3rd Earl of Egremont, was only 12 years old when he inherited Petworth, and lived for another 75 years. He was a generous, indulgent man, with a great interest in fashion, art, agriculture, and industrial development. During his lifetime, Petworth became a meeting point for many artists and intellectuals. George greatly extended the already impressive art collection, and in 1827 commissioned J. M. W. Turner to paint four glorious views of Brighton, the Chichester canal, and Petworth itself, bathed in golden sunlight. They were incorporated into the Carved Room, where they hang among older paintings and carved 17th-century decorations by Grinling Gibbons and John Seldon.

Keen to create his own temple to the arts, George began extending the North Gallery from 1824, to display his ever-increasing art collection. Probably influenced by the recently built Dulwich Picture Gallery in London, he added the top-lit Central Corridor and the large square North Bay.

Alongside antiques and neo-classical sculpture, you can find many of the greatest Georgian artists here, including Thomas Gainsborough, Angelica Kauffman, William Blake, and more Turners. The great patron himself is also present, in the form of a portrait by Thomas Phillips, who painted him sitting in this rare surviving example of an early 19th-century purpose-built art gallery.

Address Petworth House and Park, Petworth, GU28 9LR, www.nationaltrust.org.uk/visit/sussex/petworth | Getting there By train to Pulborough, then a Stagecoach connection; by car via the A283, using satnav code GU28 9LR; Compass bus 99 from Chichester | Hours (House only) Daily, but times vary during the year; check website for details | Tip Look out for the Elizabethan 'Molyneux Globe' in the East Wing of the Gallery; made by Emery Molyneux in 1592, it was the first terrestrial globe made in England.

96 Petworth Park and Garden

700 acres of 'Capability' Brown at his best

Petworth House has been managed by the National Trust since 1947, but it looks back at a long and rich history of private owners. Since the 12th century, when it was a fortified manor, it has been the seat of the Percy, Seymour, and Wyndham dynasties. The present Lord and Lady Egremont live in the private south wing of the house. While the house itself is a treasure trove of art, the surrounding 700-acre parkland is equally magnificent, with some veteran trees that are nearly 1,000 years old.

The park is home to hundreds of fallow deer, reportedly hunted by Henry VIII on a visit to Petworth in the 1520s. Later in the 16th century, Elizabethan gardens were laid out, featuring a rose garden and a fountain. Nothing of these gardens survives, but some of the outlines later formed the basis of the Pleasure Ground. In the 17th century, formal Baroque Gardens were introduced.

All this was swept away by the 2nd Earl of Egremont, who in 1751 commissioned the greatest English landscape designer, Lancelot 'Capability' Brown. He banished formality and created a great expanse of natural-looking parkland with distant views from Petworth House to the South Downs. Brown replaced straight lines with meandering paths, planted large trees and shrubs on the margin of the park, and introduced rolling slopes towards an artificial serpentine lake.

In the wooded 30-acre Pleasure Garden to the north of the house, he planted a rich variety of colourful flowering shrubs, as well as many different trees, bought from the Kensington nursery of John Williamson. An Ionic Rotunda, designed by Matthew Brettingham, was erected at a high point in the garden in 1760, while an earlier Doric Temple was moved to a lower terrace. Although the park has undergone some changes since then, it remains one of the finest and most unspoilt examples of 'Capability' Brown's work.

Address Petworth House and Park, Petworth, GU28 9LR, www.nationaltrust.org.uk/visit/sussex/petworth | **Getting there** Train to Pulborough then a Stagecoach connection (just over five miles); Compass bus 99 from Chichester; Petworth car park is on the A 283 – use satnav post code GU28 9LR | **Hours** Deer Park daily 8am – 6pm; Pleasure Garden daily 10am – 5pm | **Tip** Go for a romantic stroll and try to find the spot where J. M. W. Turner painted *Dewy Morning*, his first picture of Petworth House, or the two views of Petworth Park hanging in the Carved Room of the house.

97 __ St Mary Church
Can a spire be jinxed?

This church in the pretty Sussex village of Petworth – among Britain's leading antique trade towns – dates back to the 13th century. A church existed here, though, in Saxon times, and one is recorded in the Domesday Book. The present St Mary is linked to the murder of St Thomas Becket, as one of the chapels founded by Henry II in penance for his knights' evil 1170 deed in Canterbury Cathedral.

Today, the church provides a wonderfully atmospheric venue for concerts during the annual Petworth Festival, but it's arguably most famous for the jinx that has bedevilled all attempts at giving it a traditional pointy spire. Throughout its early centuries, it had a wood and lead steeple – but, like the tower in Pisa, this began to slant increasingly to one side. This gave rise to an old rhyme about the town: 'Proud Petworth, Poor People. / High Church, Crooked Steeple.'

The original spire became so perilously tilted that it was taken down in 1800, and replaced with an octagonal brick spire designed by Charles Barry, who was later the architect of the iconic Houses of Parliament in London. But his tower too became unstable, and was finally condemned as unsafe in 1947, leading again to demolition. After a period of architectural head scratching, the present arrangement of a parapet and low tiled roof was built – so far, remaining pleasingly vertical.

Inside, the church has a ravishing panelled wood ceiling created from 1903 to 1904 by Charles, Baron Leconfield. Elsewhere, the High Altar commemorates those killed when German bombs fell on the Boys' School in North Street in 1942. In the Baptistery, a marble female figure bears a secret message of annoyance. Feeling his talents were not fully recognised, its 19th-century creator, John Edward Carew, inscribed on the plinth: '*Fecit. Proh Pudor Academiae non Academicus*' ('To the shame of the Academy not an Academician')!

Address Church Street, Petworth, GU28 0AE, www.stmaryspetworth.co.uk | **Getting there** Petworth is 15 miles from Chichester, via the A272 and A283 | **Hours** Opening times vary, but generally Tue–Sun 9am–5pm, with extra evening openings for music | **Tip** Visit on a Thursday evening 7.30–9pm to hear the bell ringers practise on the church's peal of eight bells, cast in 1924 and tuned to a diatonic scale in the key of E.

98__Hardham Wall Paintings
Medieval marvels in a tiny rural church

Despite a little sign saying '12th Century Frescoes' by a lane off the
A29 near Pulborough, it would be all too easy to miss this startling
panoply of ancient art that would likely draw coaches of visitors if it
was somewhere like Italy. Instead, they adorn a simple, tiny church
hiding just metres from a rush of passing traffic.

Covering the interior of the 11th-century St Botolph's is one of
the most complete sets of medieval frescoes in England. They depict
some 40 scenes, loosely grouped into categories: Adam and Eve on
the chancel west wall; Christ's doings in the nave and chancel; judge-
ment and apocalypse (including Hell) across the entire west wall. A
Crusade-era depiction of St George In Battle Against The Infidel
sits low on the North and East Wall.

English medieval church frescoes were often covered with lime-
wash, meaning the Hardham paintings were only revealed during restoration work in 1866. Early conservation efforts with inappropriate
materials caused more harm than good, and improved efforts to find
the best way to save these historic art treasures from the ravages of
light, heat and moisture continue today.

1980s scientific analysis shed fascinating light on how the works
were made in a distinctive 'bacon and egg' palette – red and yellow
ochre, lime white and carbon black – that owed much to reliance on
a limited range of cheap, locally available pigments. Even the bluish
tone of the nave was made by mixing white and black.

Stylistic clues also point to the Hardham paintings being a rare
surviving example of the work of a single workshop of artists, who
travelled around Sussex in the years around 1100. Though the individual painters remain nameless, they have been dubbed the 'Lewes
Group' because of similar creations in other churches – such as
Clayton – all believed to be linked to the now-ruined Cluniac priory in Lewes.

Address Hardham Church Farm, Pulborough, RH20 1LB, www.sussexparishchurches.org |
Getting there The church is on a little lane looping off the A29, a mile south of Pulborough |
Hours Daily 9am–5pm or dusk (whichever is later) | **Tip** The Labouring Man is an excellent
country pub offering meals and rooms just off the A29, a mile south of Hardham in the
neighbouring village of Coldwaltham (www.labouringman.com).

99 Portrait of Mai
Beautiful copy of Reynolds' greatest work

In 1776, the artist Joshua Reynolds, then at the height of his career and first President of the then recently founded Royal Academy, displayed what is probably his greatest work at the Academy's summer exhibition: a full-length portrait of Mai (also known as O'Mai or Omiah), the first Pacific Islander to visit Britain, who had recently returned to the South Sea Islands. Mai had arrived in the country a couple of years earlier on the ship *Adventure*, having joined Captain Cook's second voyage in Tahiti. Mai quickly became a celebrity in Georgian society.

Reynolds' portrait is elegant, tonally stunning, and probably the first British painting to depict a non-white person with great dignity and authority. Mai's pose is based on Western Classical sculpture, but the costume is his own, and his tattoos clearly visible. The painting has always attracted attention in British art history, highlighting issues concerning colonialism and attitudes to race.

After ending up in a private collection, the original painting was sold quite recently for an eye-watering sum of £50 million. However, in recognition of its cultural importance, an export ban was put in place, and with the help of a host of sponsors, the portrait was eventually bought jointly by the Getty Trust in the US and the National Portrait Gallery in London, and now moves between these two institutions.

If you're unable to get to London or Los Angeles to see this undisputed masterpiece, Parham House has this fine copy, attributed to James Northcote, who was a contemporary of Reynolds. It takes centre stage in the Green Room, which celebrates the life and work of the botanist Sir Joseph Banks, one of Mai's patrons. To either side of Mai's portrait are copies by Ying Cheng Yang of George Stubbs' paintings of a dingo and a kangaroo, the latter being based on a kangaroo skin Banks brought back from one of his journeys.

Address Parham House & Gardens, Pulborough, RH20 4HS, +44 (0)190 374 2021,
www.parhaminsussex.co.uk | Getting there Train to Pulborough railway station; bus 100
runs to the main gate hourly Mon–Sat; by car via the A 283 – satnav post code RH20 4HR |
Hours Apr–Oct Wed, Thu, Fri, Sun & Bank Holidays; gardens noon–5pm, house 2–5pm |
Tip Parham has another portrait by Mai: he is pictured in a sepia drawing (also hanging in
the Green Room) after a painting by William Parry, showing Banks introducing Mai to the
Swedish botanist Daniel Solander; Parry was a pupil of Reynolds.

100 Pulborough Brooks Reserve

A wildlife Eden in a breathtaking landscape

Located on the floodplain of the Arun Valley with beautiful South Down views, Pulborough Brooks offers a chance to explore a kaleidoscope of landscapes, from lush grasslands and beautiful pools, to wildflower meadows and newly restored heathland. With such a dazzling variety of ecosystems, this nature reserve – overseen by the Royal Society for the Protection of Birds (RSPB) – supports a wonderful diversity of wildlife for visitors to discover throughout the year.

Book a guided night safari in June or July, for example, to hear the churring sound of nightjars flitting across the heath, while bats whirr past your head, and glow worms twinkle in the undergrowth. Arrive just before dusk, and you may see the ghostly forms of barn owls beginning to hunt over the darkening grassland. Another iconic bird here is the peregrine falcon. This fastest of all falcons makes regular appearances at Pulborough Brooks during the winter, prompting panic among the wildfowl as it hunts. Other birds of prey to scan the skies for include harriers, and the wonderfully named merlin. In between watching the ancient dance between predator and prey, admire the local widgeons, colourful ducks that gather here between October and March, whistling cheerily as they graze! Lapwings also gather in winter flocks, offering up acrobatic displays in spring as the mating season begins. In April and May, listen out for the magical song of nightingales coming from the hedgerows and scrub.

While birds may be the star turns for many visitors, the reserve offers a host of other natural wonders. Come in autumn when woodlands shimmer with brightly hued leaves, and the soil is arrayed with eye-catching fungi. Look out for the amethyst deceiver and green elf cup on the wooded heathland trail – as well as the evocatively named fairy-tale fly agaric, as bright warning red as it is deadly.

Address Wiggonholt, Pulborough, RH20 2EL, www.rspb.org.uk | Getting there The reserve is 2 miles via road and public footpath from Pulborough railway station; Compass bus 100 runs from Pulborough station to the request stop outside the reserve | Hours Daily dawn–dusk; visitor centre and café 10am–4pm | Tip The RSPB also runs the nearby Amberley Wildbrooks Reserve, a two-mile walk on the Wey-South Path from Amberley village, or by train to Amberley railway station.

101 — Wendy House at Parham
Shelter and joy in a walled garden

Parham is one of the most beautiful country houses in England and boasts many stunning features and works of art, but it would be nothing without its surrounding 875-acre estate, originally a medieval deer park.

The land was granted by King Henry VIII to Robert Palmer in 1540, and the house dates from the late 16th century. The gardens consist of seven acres of pleasure grounds, which were laid out in the 18th century, including a large pond and a brick and turf maze. Its walled garden also dates from that time, but is probably based on a much older layout, and likely pre-dates the house.

In 1922, Parham was sold to Clive and Alicia Pearson, at a time when the house and garden were in a state of disrepair. The Pearsons began a long project of renovation and re-creation of the estate, including the walled garden, which is now one of the great attractions of Parham. They introduced several new buildings, including a magnificent set of greenhouses, one of which survives.

They hired the Arts and Craft architect Victor Heal, who also worked on the restoration of the main house, to design what is perhaps the most charming of Parham's features – a Wendy House for their three daughters, built into the walls of the garden in 1928. Almost large enough to live in, this house is a child's dream, featuring a wooden floor and staircase, a working fireplace, and several rooms arranged over two floors. There is even a wrought-iron balcony.

During World War II the Pearsons welcomed dozens of evacuated children from London to Parham. The Wendy House must have given them much joy during their time there. Parham is now owned by a charitable trust, and Lady Emma Barnard and her family, who live there, are deeply involved in every aspect of its care and preservation. Traditionally, the family spends several summer nights in the Wendy House.

Address Parham House & Gardens, Pulborough, RH20 4HS, +44 (0)190 374 2021, www.parhaminsussex.co.uk | **Getting there** Train to Pulborough; bus 100 runs to the main gate hourly Mon–Sat; by car via the A283 – satnav post code RH20 4HR | **Hours** Apr–Oct Wed, Thu, Fri, Sun and Bank Holidays; gardens noon–5pm, house 2–5pm | **Tip** If you like curious brick structures, look out for Parham's late 18th-century icehouse, built into the side of Windmill Hill; ice would have been collected from ponds on the estate in the winter months and would keep in the deep structure until the summer.

102 Eric Coates Plaque

Unexpected birth of an iconic theme tune

Having adorned the BBC airwaves since 1942, *Desert Island Discs* is Britain's longest-running radio programme, with over 3,000 guests having shared their eight favourite pieces of music along with their life story, before being 'cast away' to a mythical desert island. But while the show's lilting theme – written by Eric Coates, and entitled *By The Sleepy Lagoon* – might be expected to have roots in some tropical vista, it was actually inspired by a sea view from the village of Selsey.

A blue plaque now records this quirky genesis at one end of Selsey's beachfront promenade, near where the Coates had a seaside home. Speaking to the BBC, Austin Coates recalled how his father came to write the tune in 1930, inspired 'in a very curious way' by the view on a still summer evening looking across the 'lagoon' from the east beach at Selsey towards Bognor Regis. The deep blue sea reminded Coates of the Pacific, while evening light cast a pink hue over Bognor, which made it appear to the composer 'almost like an enchanted city'. All this came together to inspire the writing of *By The Sleepy Lagoon*.

Though hailed 'The King of British Light Music', Coates was an adept classically trained musician, who played in orchestras conducted by Debussy, Elgar, Delius, Schoenberg and Vaughan Williams. Elgar admired Coates' 1919 *Summer Days* suite so much that he reputedly wore out his recording of it. In 1936, meanwhile, Coates wrote one of the earliest concert works for solo saxophone, *Saxo-Rhapsody*.

He remains best-known for 'light' compositions, including one picked up for the British 1950s film *The Dam Busters* to become 'The Dam Busters March'. In 1940, meanwhile, American lyricist Jack Lawrence wrote words for *By The Sleepy Lagoon*, and the resulting song – which Coates loved – was recorded by bigband leader Harry James, and went to number one in the Billboard charts in 1942.

212

Address East end of East Beach promenade (by Drift Lane), Selsey, PO20 0PN | Getting there Bus 51 runs from Chichester bus station to Selsey; on foot, walk from the Seal Road stop to the plaque in 20 minutes, or hop on the Selsey Circular community bus to the nearby East Beach Car Park | Hours Accessible 24 hours | Tip There's also a blue plaque on the Sussex house where Coates lived in Bognor Regis, at 6 Aldwick Avenue.

103 Pagham Harbour Reserve

Avian wonderland in a tidal landscape

One of the few undeveloped stretches of the Sussex coast is now home to an internationally recognised nature reserve, overseen by the Royal Society for the Protection of Birds (RSPB). A visitor centre offers both information and binoculars to hire to help take in the harbour's 1,500-acre tapestry of salt marshes and mudflats, complemented by grassland, copses, reed beds, lagoons and shingle. A network of footpaths helps visitors see a dazzling array of wildlife, or just soak up big sky coastal vistas.

There's a distinctive seasonality to the birdlife on view. Waders and wildfowl dominate in the autumn and winter, with large flocks of brent geese a famed arrival between September and January. Visit the harbour's north side during the winter months for the spectacle of hundreds of geese passing overhead to graze inland fields. During the summer, the harbour teems with wheatears, sand martins and chiffchaffs, complemented by black-tailed godwits and little egrets. Another summer highlight is the chattering activity around Tern Island: get a good view of common, sandwich and little terns diving for fish, by looking across the harbour from the hamlet of Church Norton.

Pagham Harbour's habitat patchwork is framed by a landscape once inhabited by both Romans and Saxons. In the Middle Ages, Pagham was a thriving port, and in the 18th century boasted one of the finest tidal mills in England, sporting three vast water wheels. The Selsey Tram from Chichester ran alongside the harbour's edge between Ferry Channel and Sidlesham between 1897 and 1935. But a terrifying 1910 storm changed the landscape dramatically, with the sea smashing through man-made defences to flood the land for miles inland. The area became an aircraft firing range during World War II, before now welcoming more peaceful winged things.

Address Pagham Harbour Nature Reserve, Selsey Road, Chichester, PO20 7NE, www.rspb.org.uk | Getting there By car, the RSPB Visitor Centre is beside the B 2145 linking Chichester and Selsey; bus 51 stops directly outside | Hours Visitor centre daily 10am–4pm; nature reserve accessible 24 hours | Tip The Crab and Lobster (www.crab-lobster.co.uk) is a fine historic gastropub by the harbour in the pretty village of Sidlesham – but don't park too close to the water's edge on an incoming tide, as the rising sea can flood the road!

104 Railway Carriage Homes
Vintage trains at a final seaside stop

Stretching back from the eastern end of Selsey's East Beach promenade is an enclave of remarkable homes – former railway carriages ingeniously recycled first as quirky holiday homes, and then permanent dwellings, clustered in an area known as the Park Estate. To see two striking examples, wander down the road running east from the Eric Coates plaque until you come to a pair of strange-looking neighbours named 'Green Bungalow' and 'Santos'. They clearly show their origins – in this case, carriages from the 1920s. So how did they come to be here?

The 1890s saw the area split into 50 plots for holiday accommodation. The railway homes, though, began appearing in the 1920s when an advertisement in the *Chichester Observer* offered 'Rail Coaches Suitable for Bungalows', with a starting price of £25 for a 5-compartment, 3rd Class carriage. Buyers wanting something more upmarket, however, could splash out on classier options, including 1890s first class compartments reconditioned by Pullman – manufacturers of luxury train carriages used across Europe on trains such as the Orient Express.

The actual sourcing of the carriages has hints of shady dealing. The Park Estate land was purchased in 1920 by an East London tailor called Jacob Berg (known to friends as Tommy), who was introduced to Selsey by a famous playwright friend, R. C. Sherriff, author of *Journey's End*. Tommy, in turn, had a friend at London's Waterloo Station. They were a likely source of the carriages – most from the London, Brighton and South East Railway (LBSER) – though details of the deal remain a mystery.

Around 30 carriage homes remain around the estate, though most now hide their origins behind clapboard encasing, added against the coastal weather. As a footnote, the whole estate was taken over during World War II to house Canadian and US soldiers just before they set off on D-Day.

Address Park Copse, Selsey, PO20 9BT | **Getting there** Bus 51 from Chichester station to Selsey, walk from the Seal Road stop to the Park Estate in 30 minutes, or hop on the Selsey Circular community bus to East Beach Road | **Hours** Exteriors accessible 24 hours | **Tip** If you'd like to stay in a railway carriage home on the Selsey seafront, you can rent Seabanks – two lovingly restored, 19th-century Stroudley railway carriages turned into a holiday let for up to eight people (www.seabankselsey.com/index.html).

105 Selsey Fishing Fleet

Make time for Britain's oldest seafood gatherers

The little flotilla of boats bobbing on the English Channel swells off Selsey's East Beach are the remainders of the oldest recorded fishing fleet in Britain. The fisher folk of Selsey – at the tip of the arrow-shaped Manhood Peninsula just south of Chichester – were first recorded by the Venerable Bede (a monk considered Britain's first true historian) writing in around A.D. 700. He described the story of St Wilfrid arriving here two decades earlier, and teaching locals how to take fish from the sea using nets.

A long promenade runs along the East Beach shingle from Selsey Bill – the southern-most point in Sussex – and around half-way along, piles of lobster and crab pots mingle with little shore boats by a cluster of huts and warehouses that are home to around half a dozen full-time crews who still ply the waters of Selsey – some dating their family fishing heritage back five centuries.

Recent archaeological finds offer evidence of the far older gathering of seafood here. During the creation of the Medmerry salt marshes west of Selsey, Chichester District Archaeologist James Kenny described the discovery of 'rows of stumps, one… in excess of 90 metres long' exposed at low tide along the shoreline. 'The oak posts had willow, poplar and other woods wound between them to make a sort of fence. Wattle was also found between the stakes,' he said. 'The conclusion was that this structure had been fish traps.' Radiocarbon dating was consistent with the structure dating back to the time of St Wilfrid.

Selsey's historic reputation for its seafood saw Elizabethan historian William Camden (after whom the London borough of Camden is named) write in 1586 how the town was 'famous for good cockles and full lobsters'. Its crab and lobster continue to be particularly prized both in the UK, and further afield in France, Portugal and Spain, and even Asia.

Address East Beach, Kingsway, Selsey, PO20 0SY | Getting there Bus 51 from Chichester station to the seafront stop at Selsey Seal Road; alternatively walk from the Seal Road stop to the fishing fleet huts in 15 minutes, or hop on the Selsey Circular community bus to the nearby East Beach car park | Hours Accessible 24 hours | Tip Buy fresh seafood at Julie's food stand amid the fishing huts, or order a fresh Selsey crab sandwich at the nearby Lifeboat Inn.

106 Selsey Lifeboat Station

Meeting place of history and fortitude

The Royal National Lifeboat Institution's 238 stations provide a 24-hour rescue service to those in trouble around Britain's vast shoreline. Staffed by brave volunteers, each station has its own raft of fascinating stories – including the one established at Selsey in 1861. Before operations began, the station's first lifeboat was taken to Chichester for its crew to show off their abilities, before being brought to Selsey, drawn by four horses. This arrival was re-enacted in 2011 on the station's 150th anniversary. The boat's first rescue saw it aid a schooner caught in gales on 23 January 1863.

Age and changing technology have seen a long line of boats in service at Selsey. The latest – the *Shannon* – is the first modern lifeboat propelled by waterjets instead of propellers, making her the world's most agile and manoeuvrable lifeboat. Launch methods have changed too. Between 1861 and 1913, lifeboats were laboriously pulled over wooden skids laid across the beach. These were replaced by slipways with rails, down which the lifeboat would slide dramatically into the sea. Station visitors can see the lifeboat up close, try on crew kit, and discover rescue stories. One World War II effort saw the Selsey boat pluck RAF Squadron-Leader J. R. A. Peel from his downed plane back to shore, from where he headed to nearby Tangmere airfield, and took to the air again just three hours after being shot down!

Over 1971 to 1975, meanwhile, the Selsey station staged the madcap International Birdman Rally. This challenged participants to compete for a £1,000 prize by throwing themselves off the high slipway – strapped into various aerial 'aids' – and 'fly' or glide at least 50 yards (46 metres) before crashing into the water… Amazingly, in 1974, David Cook almost succeeded, with a 44-metre flight – against challengers including 'Mary Poppins', 'Peter Pan' and a naked man called John!

Address The Boathouse, 154 Kingsway, Selsey, PO20 0DL, www.rnli.org | Getting there
Bus 51 runs from Chichester bus station to the seafront stop at Selsey Seal Road; walk along
the beach promenade to the Lifeboat Station in 15 minutes | Hours Visitor centre and shop
open Tue – Sat 10.30am – 4pm | Tip As well as special Open Days featuring things like boat
races and traditional sea songs, watch the lifeboat being launched – now carried down the
beach on a motorised platform – every two weeks as part of regular crew training; check
dates via www.facebook.com/SelseyRNLI.

107 St Wilfrid's Chapel

Religious beacon honouring birds and bravery

St Wilfrid's looks today like a simple cemetery chapel, but fascinating stories cling to its stones, set beside the tidal mudflats of the Pagham Harbour nature reserve. Dating to the 12th century, the building was once part of a monastery founded here in the 680s by St Wilfrid, who, after quarrelling with a Northumbrian king, sailed south to convert Sussex's pagan Saxons. The church then served as the episcopal seat for the region, its bishops holding sway for four centuries, until the Normans moved the headquarters of the bishopric to Chichester, where it remains.

Inside, recesses in the simple white stone walls present contrasting scenes. In one of them, 1530s carvings of Lord of the Manor John Lewis and his wife Agatha kneel at prayer in an image of Tudor piety. Beside it, the images are far bloodier – one has St George in dragon-slaying mode, while another shows the teenage St Agatha's torture and martyrdom by 3rd-century Roman soldiers.

More uplifting are two distinctive 20th-century stained glass windows. An inspiring 1969 window by Carl Edwards commemorates women in a host of roles – such as nursing – as well as showing an image of the now-demolished All Saints Cathedral in Cairo. A delightful 1982 window by Michael Farrar-Bell, meanwhile, celebrates the wildlife of the adjacent nature reserve.

The churchyard holds special significance for a clutch of military graves from World War I and World War II, overseen by the Commonwealth War Graves Commission. Among the fallen buried here is World War II German airman Hans Beck, shot down on 26 June 1941. His grave is Plot C, Row 8, Grave 14. The church was also the setting for the 1910 poem 'Eddi's Service' by Rudyard Kipling, reflecting on the story of a priest determined to celebrate Midnight Mass one stormy Christmas Eve, despite no parishioners attending – preaching instead to an old donkey and a weary bullock.

Address Rectory Lane, Church Norton, Chichester, PO20 9DT | Getting there The Chapel is at the end of a lane about a mile off the B 2145 between Chichester and Selsey; bus 51 runs from central Chichester | Hours Daily 10am–6pm | Tip A much larger church stood here until the 1860s, when it was decided to remove most of it brick by brick to build what is now St Peter's Church, two miles away on Selsey High Street – leaving only the old Chancel on the present site. Go to the Selsey church to see some fine features that once stood at Church Norton, including a magnificent oak roof with striking king and queen posts, and 12th-century arcades.

108__ The Wave

An icon of Japan breaking by a Sussex field

Visitors approaching Selsey on the road from Chichester are welcomed to this charming seaside town by a giant bronze sculpture of one of the most iconic images in Japanese culture – Katsushika Hokusai's *Great Wave*. Created in the 1830s as a series of prints, the image is more formally known as *The Hollow of the Deep Sea Wave off Kanagawa.*

Fashioned from blue-green bronze, and augmented by pebbles from Selsey beach, this two-metre bronze is by William Pye, famed for works that celebrate water in some way. Cast in 2000 for an exhibition in London of works paying homage to another artist, the piece was then put on display at the Cass Sculpture Foundation a few miles north of Chichester, until its sad closure in 2020 saw the piece moved beside lush Sussex fields at the entrance to Selsey.

Though the artistic image that inspired the piece depicts stormy waters off Japan, Pye also took cues from the New York coast. 'The beginnings of this project can be traced many years ago to a moment when I became fascinated by massive waves crashing on the Long Island shore, while staying with friends,' he said. 'I thought about how the fleeting life of these impressive forms might be captured sculpturally.'

Also a film-maker and musician, Pye took up sculpting at the age of 12, going on to study at London's prestigious Royal College of Art in the 1960s. Galleries holding his work include New York's Museum of Modern Art, and he has more sculptures on view in public in London than any other modern British sculptor. Hokusai's 'wave' series – featuring Mount Fuji in the background – was introduced to the European market in the mid 19th century, and has become an emblem of Japan's artistic heritage. The exact number of prints he produced remains a mystery, however, as does the number that still exist. But we know there is only one sculpture like *The Wave.*

Address Roundabout by the junction of Chichester Road and Manor Road at the entrance to Selsey, PO20 0NL | Getting there Bus 51 from Chichester to either ASDA or Golf Links Lane | Hours Accessible 24 hours | Tip Wave-lovers should head a few miles west to the beaches of the Witterings, a year-round Sussex hotspot for surfing and windsurfing; East Wittering surf shop Shore offers tuition and board rental (www.shore.co.uk).

109 Slindon Cricket Memorial

The global sport born in a Sussex village

Cricket has global appeal. The 2023 Men's Cricket World Cup in India saw teams from countries like Afghanistan and the Netherlands battle leading nations such as Australia and England, while the sport will return to the Olympic Games for Los Angeles 2028. But in the little Sussex village of Slindon, a striking bat-and-ball memorial acknowledges its claim to be the birthplace of the game.

The 2.8 metre wooden memorial by Slindon Common nods to a match played here in 1731, which saw the formulation of the rules that underpin today's global sport. Matches are still played on the common, and as local players stride to the crease they can reflect on the 1740 match, when 'poore little Slyndon' defeated a team of England's finest players in a result as pleasingly unexpected as when Afghanistan beat reigning champions, England, at the 2023 Men's World Cup!

The roots of cricket in the sheep-grazing folds of the Sussex landscape go back even further, however. The sport is widely believed to have originated from locals bowling a ball of wool or rags at a target – such as the gate of a sheep pasture – which was defended with a bat in the form of a shepherd's crooked staff. A 14th-century mural in Cocking Church near Chichester depicts shepherds carrying wooden cricks very like improvised bats. And in 1622 complaints were made to the Bishop of Chichester about men in the village of Boxgrove – four miles from Slindon – breaking church windows by playing cricket in the churchyard!

Cricket as an organised sport also owes much to 17th century employees on the nearby Goodwood estate – including many from Slindon – who challenged local landowners. Slindon Common was an ideal venue, as its surface of clay on gravel offered a faster, more level pitch than downland turf. Howzat!

Address Junction of Reynolds Lane and Park Lane, Slindon, BN18 0QT | Getting there By car via the A27 and A29 | Hours Accessible 24 hours | Tip The Forge is a community-owned café, shop and information centre fashioned from an old 19th-century workshop, a stone's throw from the Memorial (www.slindonforge.co.uk).

110_ Tangmere Aviation Museum

Unforgettable reminders of Air Force heroes

Having served as an RAF fighter station from 1918 to 1958, Tangmere is the perfect location for this stirring museum, opened in 1982 to promote public awareness of Britain's military aviation heritage, along with poignant reminders of the price sometimes paid by those serving their country. There's a spectacular array of aircraft from different generations. Some of the most historic are on view in the grounds, including a Phantom FGR2, Sea Harrier and Harrier GR3. The Meryl Hansed Memorial Hall, meanwhile, spotlights preservation work on two classic planes: a Hunter Mk 5 and an English Electric Lightning F 53.

Merston Hall is home to two world airspeed record-breaking aircraft – Donaldson's Meteor and Duke's Hunter – both on loan from the RAF Museum. They sit alongside a Hurricane – a key player in the Battle of Britain – and a full-sized replica of the Spitfire prototype K 5054. Immersive offerings include flight simulators, plus an Air Raid Experience set within a World War II air raid shelter from the original RAF airfield. This provides full sound effects of a bombing raid that hit Tangmere on 16 August 1940.

The human side of air war is movingly remembered in exhibits chronicling figures such as James Nicolson, the only Fighter Command pilot to be awarded the VC during World War II, while Middle Hall spotlights the vital role played by Czech and Polish squadrons who flew from Tangmere. Tributes are also paid to the Women's Auxiliary Air Force (the WAAF) and Air Transport Auxiliary (ATA), as well as the work of special agents who undertook incredibly perilous undercover missions into occupied territory, and the brave pilots who flew them there. There's also a section on the Royal Flying Corps – pioneering forerunner of the RAF – plus cultural offerings including poems written by airmen during the war years, and a gallery of aviation paintings.

Address Gamecock Terrace, Tangmere, near Chichester, PO20 2ES, www.tangmere-museum.org.uk | Getting there By car via the A 27; bus 55 runs to Tangmere | Hours Daily Mar–Oct 10am–5pm; Feb & Nov 10am–4pm | Tip In the neighbouring village of Oving, the Gribble Inn is a cosy 16th-century pub with its own on-site brewery, fashioned from the former home of village school teacher Rose Gribble (www.gribbleinn.co.uk).

111_West Wittering Beach

Secluded beacon of screen stars and wild nature

You might expect a beach that has provided the backdrop for a role call of A-list screen stars to be located somewhere like California, or at least in an exotic tropical paradise. But at the tip of Chichester Harbour is an expanse of sand backed with picture-perfect dunes, and it's this that has provided the location for movies starring such luminaries as Michelle Williams and Ewan McGregor (*Incendiary*), Dakota Fanning (*Now Is Good*), and Colin Firth, Jude Law and Nicole Kidman (*Genius*). The production team for aristocratic TV drama *Downton Abbey* also visited to shoot scenes for a 2013 seaside special.

A more recent big screen outing came in 2019, when West Wittering beach stood in for the exclusive US East Coast enclave The Hamptons for the drama *Blackbird*, starring Susan Sarandon, Sam Neill and Kate Winslet – though another reason for the location choice was that Winslet lives here! She even convinced a neighbour to rent out their showstopper modern home to provide the film's primary domestic location.

Sometimes nicknamed God's Pocket by locals thanks to a microclimate considered balmy for England, this shore is also popular with a less starry set of water sports fans, as well as bird-lovers attracted by a pleasing plethora of water birds. If nature's your passion, walk west along the beach to reach East Head, an atmospheric wild enclave where Chichester Harbour opens into the English Channel.

There are rock and roll links here too. The legendary 1970s rock opera *Tommy*, featuring Elton John and Tina Turner along with The Who, rolled cameras here, while Rolling Stones' guitarist Keith Richards is another local star resident. It was at Richards' house, Redlands – tucked away up a quiet Wittering lane – that he and Mick Jagger were busted for drugs in a 1967 police raid, and put on trial in what provided one of the seminal events of 1960s cultural history.

Address West Wittering Beach car park, Pound Road, West Wittering, Chichester, PO20 8AU | Getting there Seven miles south of Chichester via the A 286; bus 52/53 runs from Chichester bus station and Cathedral | Hours West Wittering Beach and East Head accessible 24 hours | Tip For upmarket dining, The Wittering is a local gastropub showcasing produce from local suppliers (www.thewittering.com); for a more laidback vibe, head to Drifters, a family-run beachside café in the neighbouring village of East Wittering (www.drifters-ew.co.uk).

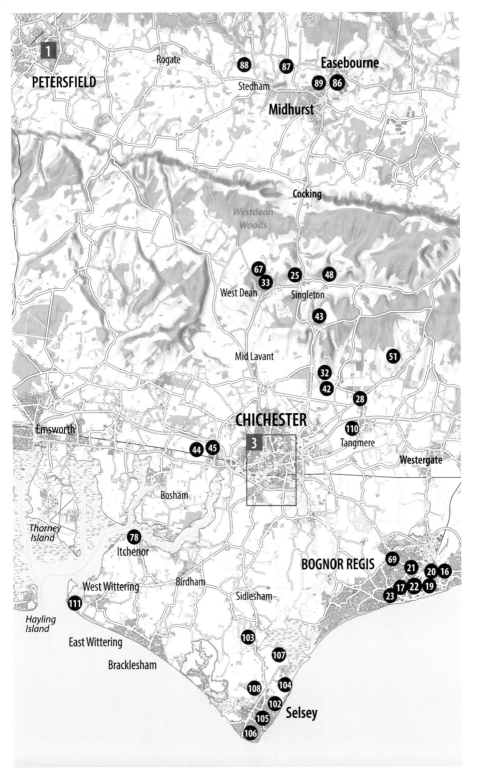

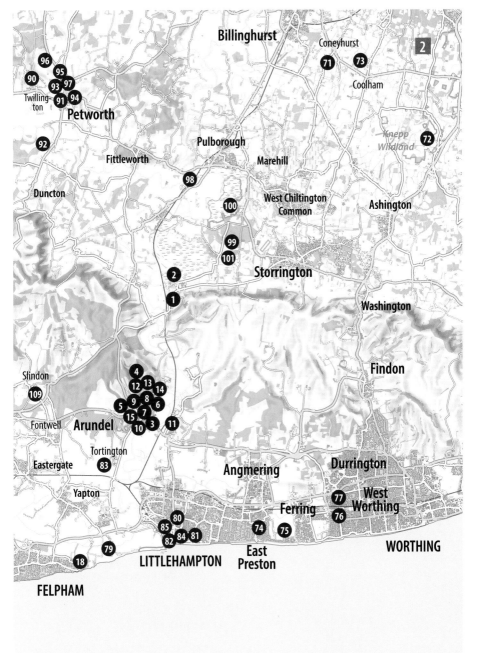

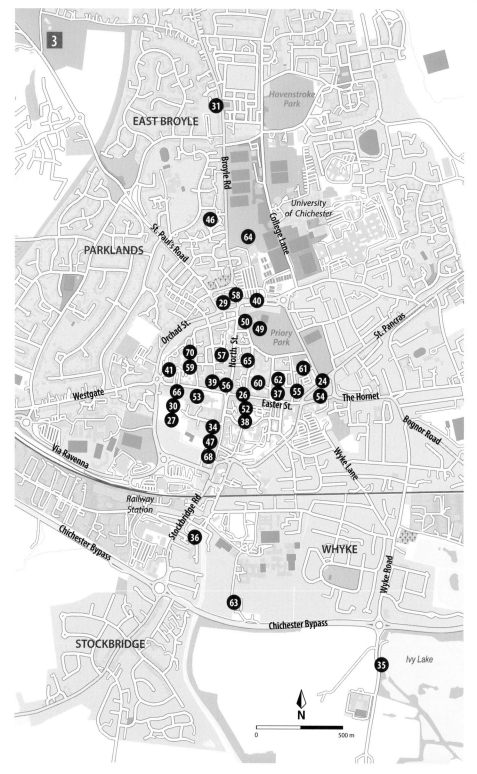

Alexandra Loske
111 Places in Brighton and Lewes That You Shouldn't Miss
ISBN 978-3-7408-1727-5

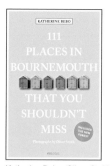

Katherine Bebo, Oliver Smith
111 Places in Bournemouth That You Shouldn't Miss
ISBN 978-3-7408-1166-2

Katherine Bebo, Oliver Smith
111 Places in Poole That You Shouldn't Miss
ISBN 978-3-7408-0598-2

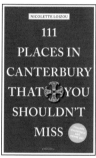

Nicolette Loizou
111 Places in Canterbury That You Shouldn't Miss
ISBN 978-3-7408-0899-0

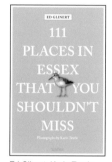

Ed Glinert, Karin Tearle
111 Places in Essex That You Shouldn't Miss
ISBN 978-3-7408-1593-6

Ed Glinert, David Taylor
111 Places in Yorkshire That You Shouldn't Miss
ISBN 978-3-7408-1167-9

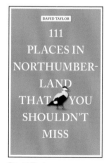

David Taylor
111 Places in Northumberland That You Shouldn't Miss
ISBN 978-3-7408-1792-3

Ed Glinert, David Taylor
111 Places in Oxford That You Shouldn't Miss
ISBN 978-3-7408-1990-3

John Sykes, Birgit Weber
111 Places in London That You Shouldn't Miss
ISBN 978-3-7408-1644-5

Solange Berchemin,
Martin Dunford, Karin Tearle
**111 Places in Greenwich
That You Shouldn't Miss**
ISBN 978-3-7408-1107-5

David Taylor
**111 Places in Newcastle
That You Shouldn't Miss**
ISBN 978-3-7408-1043-6

David Taylor
**111 Places along Hadrian's Wall
That You Shouldn't Miss**
ISBN 978-3-7408-1425-0

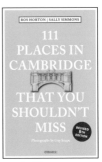

Rosalind Horton,
Sally Simmons, Guy Snape
**111 Places in Cambridge
That You Shouldn't Miss**
ISBN 978-3-7408-1285-0

Phil Lee, Rachel Ghent
**111 Places in Nottingham
That You Shouldn't Miss**
ISBN 978-3-7408-2261-3

Ben Waddington, Janet Hart
**111 Places in Birmingham
That You Shouldn't Miss**
ISBN 978-3-7408-2268-2

Solange Berchemin
**111 Places in the Lake District
That You Shouldn't Miss**
ISBN 978-3-7408-1861-6

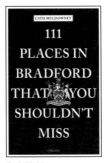

Cath Muldowney
**111 Places in Bradford
That You Shouldn't Miss**
ISBN 978-3-7408-1427-4

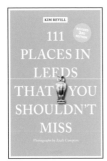

Kim Revill, Alesh Compton
**111 Places in Leeds
That You Shouldn't Miss**
ISBN 978-3-7408-0754-2

Michael Glover,
Richard Anderson
**111 Places in Sheffield
That You Shouldn't Miss**
ISBN 978-3-7408-2348-1

Julian Treuherz,
Peter de Figueiredo
**111 Places in Manchester
That You Shouldn't Miss**
ISBN 978-3-7408-2246-0

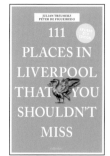

Julian Treuherz,
Peter de Figueiredo
**111 Places in Liverpool
That You Shouldn't Miss**
ISBN 978-3-7408-1607-0

Rob Ganley, Ian Williams
**111 Places in Coventry
That You Shouldn't Miss**
ISBN 978-3-7408-1044-3

Martin Booth, Barbara Evripidou
**111 Places in Bristol
That You Shouldn't Miss**
ISBN 978-3-7408-2001-5

Martin Booth, Barbara Evripidou
**111 Places for Kids in Bristol
That You Shouldn't Miss**
ISBN 978-3-7408-1665-0

Justin Postlethwaite
**111 Places in Bath
That You Shouldn't Miss**
ISBN 978-3-7408-0146-5

Gillian Tait
**111 Places in Edinburgh
That You Shouldn't Miss**
ISBN 978-3-7408-1476-2

Tom Shields, Gillian Tait
**111 Places in Glasgow
That You Shouldn't Miss**
ISBN 978-3-7408-2237-8

Photo Credits

Cedar of Lebanon (ch. 32): courtesy Goodwood House

Chalk Stone Trail (ch. 33): courtesy Alexandra Loske

Egyptian Room at Goodwood (ch. 42): courtesy Clive Boursnell/
Goodwood House

Elisabeth Frink's Horse (ch. 43): courtesy Jill Howgate/Goodwood
House

Fox Hall (ch. 48): courtesy John Miller/The Landmark Trust

John Piper Tapestry (ch. 53): courtesy © The Piper Estate/
VG Bild-Kunst, Bonn 2024

North Bersted Man (ch. 59): courtesy Peter Langdown
Photography for The Novium Museum

Knepp Rewilding Estate (ch. 72): courtesy Knepp Rewilding
Estate

Itchenor Boat Trips (ch. 78): courtesy Jenny Hinton

Bailiffscourt Hotel (ch. 79): courtesy Sophie Tanner at Historic
Sussex Hotels

Glasshouse at Woolbeding (ch. 87): courtesy Raquel Diniz/
Heatherwick Studio

Iping Common (ch. 88): courtesy Simon Smith/Sussex Wildlife
Trust

Newlands House Gallery (ch. 91): courtesy Christopher Ison/Scott
& Co

Petworth House North Gallery (ch. 95): courtesy Alexandra Loske

Petworth Park and Garden (ch. 96): courtesy Alexandra Loske

Portrait of Mai (ch. 99): courtesy Jonathan James Wilson/Parham
House

Pulborough Brooks Reserve (ch. 100): courtesy Andy Hay/Royal
Society for the Protection of Birds

Wendy House at Parham (ch. 101): courtesy Jonathan James
Wilson/Parham House

Pagham Harbour Reserve (ch. 103): courtesy Ben Andrew/Royal
Society for the Protection of Birds

Acknowledgements

There are many people I would like to thank for their support in creating this book, beginning with Laura Olk at Emons for patient guidance through the writing process, and to Martin Sketchley for his editing. Thanks also to a host of people who have provided help at several of the places I've had the pleasure to highlight in this book. They include: Oliver Tubb and Chloe Webb (Chichester Cathedral), Mike Bennett (Tangmere Aviation Museum), Alice Johnson (RSPB), Ann Stevens (Amberley Museum), Kim Standish (Edes House), David Wise (Parham House), Clementine de la Poer Beresford (Goodwood), Emily Knight (Petworth House), Melanie Edge (St Michael's, Amberley), Amanda Reeves (Sussex Wildlife Trust), Raquel Fonseca (for Newlands Gallery), Sam Beard (Horse Guards Inn), Rachel Greaves (Knepp Estate), and the team at Fishbourne Roman Palace. Last, but definitely not least, I must thank my wife Jessica, for driving me when trains or buses weren't an option!

A note on transport

Walking has been highlighted completely within the compact historic core of Chichester, while elsewhere, public transport is given prominence wherever possible. There are fast train links from Chichester to key neighbouring towns including Arundel, Littlehampton and Bognor Regis, while an excellent local bus network – from either Chichester Bus Station or Chichester Cathedral – provides car-free access to almost everywhere featured outside the city. Road routes are provided throughout the book, however – though only foregrounded for the few places where driving really is the most practical option.

Norman Miller is an award-winning journalist for leading outlets including the BBC, *The Times* and *The Guardian*, writing about an eclectic range of subjects such as travel, food and drink, history, arts and culture, and the environment. He is also a published and performed creative writer of theatre, poetry and short stories. He's contributed to several non-fiction titles, including the BBC series book *Plants: From Roots to Riches* and the photography showcase *London: The Panoramas*.

Alexandra Loske is a British-German art historian and museum curator with a particular interest in late eighteenth and early nineteenth century European art and architecture. She has been working at the University of Sussex since 1999 and at the Royal Pavilion in Brighton since 2008. She has lectured and published widely on colour history and other topics, appeared as an art historian on many TV and radio programmes and writes regularly for local and national magazines.

The information in this book was accurate at the time of publication, but it can change at any time. Please confirm the details for the places you're planning to visit before you head out on your adventures.